IMAGES
of America

THE NAVAL WAR COLLEGE

CONFERENCE OF THE AMERICAS, 1971. The front of the Naval War College is flanked with the flags of member nations attending the annual conference at the college in Newport. (Courtesy Naval War College Museum.)

IMAGES
of America

THE NAVAL WAR COLLEGE

Lionel D. Wyld

ARCADIA
PUBLISHING

ISBN 978-0-7385-0290-8

Published by Arcadia Publishing
Charleston, South Carolina

Printed in the United States of America

Library of Congress Catalog Card Number: 2009923815

For all general information contact Arcadia Publishing at:
Telephone 843-853-2070
Fax 843-853-0044
E-mail sales@arcadiapublishing.com
For customer service and orders:
Toll-Free 1-888-313-2665

Visit us on the Internet at www.arcadiapublishing.com

Also by Lionel D. Wyld

Low Bridge! Folklore and the Erie Canal
Walter D. Edmonds, Storyteller
Boaters and Broomsticks. Tales & Historical Lore of the Erie Canal
The Navy in Newport
Canastota and Chittenango: Two Historic Canal Towns

***Cover:* The Naval War College.** This 1963 view of the college shows Luce Hall in the center and Pringle Hall on the left. Completed in 1892 as the first new authorized construction for the college, the main building was later named Luce Hall in honor of the college founder and its first president, Commodore Stephen B. Luce. Pringle Hall, the addition, opened in 1934 and was named for Rear Adm. Joel Roberts Poinsett Pringle, college president from 1927 to 1930. (Naval War College Museum.)

Contents

INTRODUCTION

It is appropriate that the Navy's pioneer training station and principal graduate college was established at Newport, Rhode Island. Known as the City by the Sea, Newport has a long history of maritime activity. Newport Harbor and Narragansett Bay have always been safe and deep havens for naval as well as commercial shipping; and as far back as the Colonial period, Newport was recognized as an important seaport for the mercantile trade and a harbor of inestimable value for naval vessels.

When Commodore Stephen B. Luce established the Naval Training Station on Coasters Harbor Island in Newport in 1883, the facility was the forerunner of the modern recruit training stations for enlisted men in the Navy. The next year, 1884, Luce established the Naval War College, the first professional naval educational center of its kind in the world. Its original home was a building that previously housed the Newport asylum or poorhouse, conveniently out of the way of the town, across a small water barrier from the island. Today, a registered National Historic Landmark, that original building is Founders Hall, the Naval War College Museum.

The Naval War College soon became the U.S. Navy's premier institution for professional studies of warfare, international law, and statesmanship relating to war and peace. Among others, Luce brought to the college Capt. Alfred Thayer Mahan, a naval historian who wrote the book *The Influence of Sea Power Upon History, 1660–1783* at the college. That book and other works influenced naval thought throughout the world.

In 1894, war-gaming was added to the curriculum and the first naval war games were played at the Naval War College at Newport. This innovation, along with exceptional academic standards, brought a new level of sophistication to professional graduate education for officers in the Navy and other branches of the service. In addition to creating and maintaining an outstanding graduate school, Luce, Mahan, and their successors, along with the staff and students who have come to the Naval War College to teach and study over the years, have played an important, active part in college growth as well as the social and cultural life of the college and the Newport area.

The first authorized new construction at the college was a building for class and administration that opened in 1892. For more than ten years, that building—later to be named Luce Hall after the founder—*was* the War College. Mahan Hall was added in 1903 to provide needed library space, and two additions were added subsequently. Pringle Hall, adjacent to the original construction, was completed in 1934. The conversion of a barracks of the training station was completed in 1947 and became Sims Hall. The energetic plans of two presidents—Vice Adm. John T. Hayward and Vice Adm. Richard G. Colbert—resulted in a major facilities growth in the 1970s, with the completion of Spruance Hall in 1971, Conolly Hall in 1974, and Hewitt Hall in 1976. Also in the 1970s, the college's original home, the former poorhouse building, was again made available to the Naval War College and became Founders Hall, dedicated in 1978 as the Naval War College Museum. After intense remodeling of the entire building, the museum opened to provide ongoing support to college staff and students, and to offer the public both permanent displays and changing historical exhibits. In October 1997, a ground-breaking ceremony signaled the way for McCarty Little Hall, providing for a new Strategic Maritime Research Center with facilities for state-of-the-art war-gaming, a Strategic Studies Group, and a Decision Support Center, along with classrooms and administrative space.

The Naval War College is fully accredited by the New England Association of Schools and Colleges to award qualified resident U.S. graduates a master of arts degree in national security and strategic studies. Graduates from both of the international programs, as well as those of the College of Continuing Education, receive a Naval War College diploma.

Naval War College takes a look at one of the country's most prestigious service schools and provides a pictorial record of its historic and continuing role.

One

Beginnings: The Early Years

The Naval War College was the first professional senior naval educational center of its kind in the world. Founded in 1884 and still in operation today, it is also the oldest of its kind. In historic retrospect, it seems quite appropriate that this pioneer naval college was established in Newport, Rhode Island, a relatively small city in a very small state, with both city and state having a long history of maritime activity. The harbor at Newport has been a deep and safe haven for commercial shipping as well as naval forces since Colonial days.

The original home of the Naval War College was, to say the least, unprepossessing—an alms house for the poor of Newport city, built in the early 1800s on Coasters Harbor Island, an offshore island that was linked to the city only by a causeway. The previous year, 1883, Commodore Stephen Bleecker Luce had established the Naval Training Station on the island just outside Newport, and the next year, in 1884, he founded the Naval War College. The original building, which at various times served the Naval Training Station administration, is today a Registered Historic National Landmark.

Political foes of the Naval War College succeeded in driving the college out of the building and off the island, where the college had a short relationship with the country's pioneer Naval Torpedo Station, established in 1869 on Goat Island in Newport Harbor. In 1892, however, the college returned to Coasters Harbor Island to a newly authorized academic building, now known as Luce Hall, just west of its first home. With the college's return, the former poorhouse became the property of the Naval Training Station.

Commodore Luce was assigned as first president of the college and is remembered in the name given the building, which was the first Congress-approved new construction for the Naval War College on Coasters Harbor Island. The building was not officially named Luce Hall until 1974. At the beginning of the 20th century, the college settled down to a more or less normal running graduate college for senior naval officers. In 1898, it shut down from March 22 to November 2 on account of America's participation in the Spanish-American War. It was also closed from April 28, 1917, to April 11, 1919, because of World War I.

In these early years, the Naval War College saw a number of historically prominent persons on stage at convocations or other sessions, including Theodore Roosevelt, who came first as assistant secretary of the navy and, later, as President when he was in Newport for the Battleship Conference in 1906; Commodore Stephen Bleecker Luce, the founder; and Capt. Alfred Thayer Mahan, the naval historian and theorist. Until Mahan Hall was constructed in 1903 as a library facility, all college activities were centered in the first new building that was authorized for the fledgling college, Luce Hall, completed in 1892, while the college's original home building, the old almshouse, served as Naval Training Station headquarters and was the administration building for the station and, eventually, other commands.

COASTERS HARBOR ISLAND, C. 1832. This offshore island where the founders of Newport landed in 1639 is 2 miles north of the center of the present city. In 1883, the Naval Training Station was established on the island and the Newport Asylum for the Poor, shown here, became the first home of the Naval War College, founded in 1884. The poorhouse was built by Benjamin Chase of Newport, chiefly of fieldstone from the island, at a cost of $6,940. Work on the building began in 1817 and was completed in March 1820. The Navy acquired the building in 1881. (Naval War College Museum.)

STEREOSCOPIC VIEW OF THE NEWPORT ASYLUM FOR THE POOR, C. 1873. A front porch was added in 1878. The building was sold to the Navy in 1881 and used as the first home for the new Naval War College. (Naval War College Museum.)

NAVAL TRAINING STATION, C. 1883. This photograph was taken shortly after the activity was established. Beyond the marine sentry, at the top of the hill, is the former Newport poorhouse, which was to become home to the Naval War College, founded the next year, in 1884. The building became Naval Training Station property again in 1889 and served as the station headquarters. Many years later, in 1973, the building again became available to the college and was used to house a Naval War College museum, offering displays and exhibits on the history of naval warfare and the naval heritage of Narragansett Bay. (Courtesy A.S. Nicolosi, Director, Naval War College Museum.)

NAVAL WAR COLLEGE, C. 1884. Coasters Harbor Island became Navy property after the Naval Apprentice System squadron under Capt. Stephen Bleecker Luce's command visited Newport and subsequently the Naval Training Station was established on the island. The following year the former Newport Asylum for the Poor, built on the island 1816–1820, became home to the new Naval War College, the first school of its kind in the world. (Naval War College Museum.)

COMMODORE STEPHEN BLEECKER LUCE. A graduate of the U.S. Naval Academy, Class of 1847, Luce established the Naval Training Station in Newport in 1883 and founded the Naval War College the next year. Secretary of the Navy William E. Chandler assigned Luce "to duty as president of the college." (Copy of painting courtesy of U.S. Naval Academy, Special Collections and Archives Division, William W. Jeffries Memorial Archives.)

NAVAL HISTORY IN NEWPORT: USS CONSTITUTION. Often referred to as "Old Ironsides," the *Constitution* served as a training ship of the Naval Apprentice System in the 1870s, when the system was commanded by Capt. Stephen B. Luce. The ship and others of the training squadron came to Newport in 1880, when Coasters Harbor Island became the site of a naval training station, and then in 1884, when the Naval War College opened here. A U.S. Naval Academy school ship in 1860, Old Ironsides first came to Newport during the Civil War period. When war threatened, the Naval Academy superintendent used this ship to transport midshipmen to Newport, where the academy was relocated during the war. Arriving on May 9, 1861, the ship received a 24-gun salute from Fort Adams as it entered Newport harbor. This drawing by John Charles Roach for the *Naval War College Review* depicts a classic view of the veteran sailing ship that has historic connections to Newport and Boston, where it is now berthed. (*Naval War College Review.*)

NAVAL TRAINING STATION, COASTERS HARBOR ISLAND, C. 1888. This photograph shows a view of marching naval apprentice recruits, and the USS *New Hampshire*, an apprentice quarters ship and Naval Training Station headquarters until 1889. It also shows Barracks A, which was a drill hall built in 1883 and destroyed by fire in 1906, and another ship of the training squadron in the distance. (Courtesy A.S. Nicolosi, Director, Naval War College Museum.)

ENTRANCE TO THE NEWPORT NAVAL STATION, C. 1890. The Naval Training Station of 1890 had a pastoral look about it, as this early photograph attests. The sentry house at the end of the causeway leading from Newport was upgraded from what it had been in 1883, but nothing else appears to have changed. At this time the former poorhouse at the top of the hill, the original site of the Naval War College from 1884 to 1889, is Naval Training Station headquarters. (Courtesy A.S. Nicolosi, Director, Naval War College Museum.)

Naval War College. A *fin de siècle* view of the building completed in 1892 that later became Luce Hall, the first new construction building of the Naval War College. At the time this photograph was taken in 1898, it was the only building of the college, since the original almshouse building was taken over by the Naval Training Station, Newport, for administration in 1889. (Naval War College Museum.)

Luce Hall Circular Observatory. The cupola, originally called the circular observatory, was built for the Naval War College in the Flemish style, in 1891–92. (Courtesy *Naval War College Review*.)

Admiral Mahan. Capt. Alfred Thayer Mahan was selected by founder and first president Commodore Stephen Bleecker Luce as his successor. Mahan, who later became a rear admiral, served as president of the Naval War College at Newport for two periods: 1886–89 and 1892–93. This painting of Mahan in flag rank was done by Alexander James in 1946 and hangs in the College Conference Center in Mahan Hall on the campus. (Naval War College Museum.)

The Naval Strategy Board in Consultation at Washington. The board included Capt. A.T. Mahan, Capt. A.S. Crowninshield, Secretary of the Navy John D. Long, and Rear Adm. Montgomery Sicard. (Painted by T.V. Chrominski from a photograph by Berte & Pullis; courtesy R.M. Cembrola, Curator, Naval War College Museum.)

SCENES AT THE NAVAL WAR COLLEGE, NEWPORT, 1895. Sketches in the *New York Herald* of July 21, 1895, included the Naval War College building; Capt. H.C. Taylor, president; a torpedo firing exercise; and the Class of 1895. (Courtesy Naval War College Archives.)

Students and Staff of 1894. Naval War College president Capt. Henry Taylor, in the center of the second row, poses with the staff and the students for a class picture in 1894. On the right are officers from Sweden, the first foreign officers to attend the college. (Naval War College Museum.)

Assistant Secretary of the Navy Theodore Roosevelt and the Class of 1897. Roosevelt, in the front center, is shown with college president Cmdr. Caspar Goodrich, the staff, and the Class of 1897. Roosevelt became associated with the college in 1886 when he delivered a lecture on his successful book of the War of 1812. He returned to the college in 1906 to open the Battleship Conference held there. (Naval War College Museum.)

CLASS OF 1896. On hand for this class photograph were college president Capt. Henry Taylor, the staff, the students, and college founder Commodore Stephen Bleecker Luce, in civilian clothes on the right. (Naval War College Museum.)

Naval War College Staff and Class of 1902. College president Capt. French E. Chadwick is seated second from right. This view is particularly interesting as it shows college founder Commodore Stephen Bleecker Luce, at right center, together with Capt. F.W. Dickens, a former Naval Training Station commander and adversary of the Naval War College, at left center. When the photograph was taken, Dickens was a Naval War College student. (Naval War College Museum.)

Naval War College, c. 1905. The first new construction of the Naval War College, later named Luce Hall in honor of founder Stephen Bleecker Luce, makes a dramatic scene for a period postcard in the collection of the Naval War College Museum.

NAVAL WAR COLLEGE AND NAVAL TRAINING STATION, NEWPORT, 1906. This waterfront photograph shows the Naval War College on the hill at the left, the station administration building that was the Naval War College building in 1884, the commandant's quarters, the training ship *Constellation*, and the marine barracks. (Naval War College Museum.)

NAVAL WAR COLLEGE, c. 1908. This view includes the Naval War College in the left background, the Naval Training Station headquarters building that is now the Naval War College Museum, and the training ships *Cumberland* and *Reine Mercedes*. The photograph was taken from Green Park. (Courtesy of A.S. Nicolosi, Director, Naval War College Museum.)

NAVAL WAR COLLEGE, c. 1910–1914. Recruits of the Naval Training Station, Newport, drill on Dewey Field in front of the first new construction building of the Naval War College, founded in 1884. The building was later designated Luce Hall. (Naval War College Museum.)

Naval War College Summer Conference, 1911. When this photograph was taken, Capt. W.S. Sims, front left, was a student in the Class of 1911. Sims later served as president of the college, during World War I and again from 1919 to 1922. (Naval War College Museum.)

Naval War College and Naval Training Station, Newport, 1914. A Sunday recruit parade on Dewey Field draws visitors. Note the bow of the station training ship USS *Constellation* and the battleship fleet in the bay. (Naval War College Museum.)

NAVAL WAR COLLEGE, c. 1914. Naval Training Station recruits drill on Dewey Field in front of the Naval War College building. (Naval War College Museum.)

NAVAL WAR COLLEGE CLASS, 1914. Secretary of the Navy Josephus Daniels, in the front center, joins the Class of 1914 for this photograph. Daniels is shown with college president Rear Adm. Austin Knight and Capt. William S. Sims, with the armband, seated on right. (Naval War College Museum.)

President Sims. As a captain, William Snowden Sims served as Naval War College president from February through April 1917, when the activities of the college were temporarily discontinued on account of the participation of the United States in World War I. Later as a rear admiral, Sims served as president again, from April 1919 to October 1922. (Naval War College Museum.)

Staff and Students, 1919. Rear Adm. William Snowden Sims, president of the college, is shown with members of the staff and student body of 1919. (Naval War College Museum.)

Naval Torpedo Station, Newport, 1919. Torpedo boats line up at the Goat Island slip after World War I. The Naval War College is on the right in the distance, across the water on Coasters Harbor Island. (Courtesy NUWC Newport Graphics Division.)

Two

BUILDINGS AND FACILITIES I: EARLY CONSTRUCTION AND GROWTH

The first home of the Naval War College was a building previously known as the Newport Asylum for the Poor, completed in 1820. The former poorhouse was in a sorry state when the Navy took it over, and college founder and first president Commodore Stephen B. Luce made adapting it to academic needs a key focus of his administration. His handpicked successor, Capt. Alfred Thayer Mahan, became president in 1886. For the next three years, Mahan administered the college while he and his family lived in the same building. As circumstances required, Mrs. Mahan and their children routinely vacated portions of their living space for study purposes when school was in session.

The college left the site in 1889, merged for a short time with the pioneer Naval Torpedo Station on Goat Island in Newport Harbor, and then returned to Coasters Harbor Island in 1892 and occupied a newly built academic building located just west of its first home.

The first authorized new construction at the Naval War College, eventually named Luce Hall in honor of the college founder, was situated on Coasters Harbor Island on the bluff just west of the original college building, overlooking Narragansett Bay. This structure served as the principal college building through two wars, the Spanish-American War, 1898, and World War I, 1917–18, although the college was shut down during the actual war periods.

In the 1890s, the original building became headquarters for the Naval Training Station, which had been founded on Coasters Harbor Island the year before the Naval War College, and Luce Hall served adequately for some 40 years until an adjacent building, Pringle Hall, was constructed in 1934 on the west end. Among other things, the wings of the original building served as officers' quarters for the college's students until 1919. Mahan Hall was added in 1903 just to the rear of the original Navy-authorized college structure. Named after the college's second president and renown naval historian Alfred Thayer Mahan, the hall provided needed space for a library and archives.

Further physical expansion was limited in the interwar period, and during World War II much of Coasters Harbor Island and adjacent naval properties, such as Coddington Cove, exploded with facilities for wartime naval recruit training and housing. The college strained to meet wartime needs with its complement of buildings, as Vice Adm. William S. Pye, president of the college from November 1942 to March 1946, established the wartime command and preparatory staff courses at the college. Through its intensified and accelerated wartime program, the college provided advanced training to more than 600 naval officers. Pye also had a dual assignment as commandant of the Naval Operating Base, 1942–44, which thus put the Naval War College president in charge of all wartime operations throughout Narragansett Bay.

The conversion of a training station building, Barracks C, to Sims Hall in 1947 began the further expansion of the college campus. In the ensuing postwar decades, the college's programs and student body continued expanding and facilities were strained to keep pace with the institution, which was becoming both more diversified and of increasing importance in defense training. During the Cold War, the college trained senior officers of the U.S. Navy, Marine Corps, and Coast Guard in naval warfare and the attendant areas of global strategy, maritime leadership, and international diplomacy.

Original Naval War College Building. This 1925 photograph shows the original home of the Naval War College when it was founded in 1884. The 1820 building later served as headquarters of the Naval Training Station, Newport, and still later became the home of the Naval War College Museum. (Naval War College Museum.)

Naval War College, c. 1913. The first new construction authorized for the Naval War College, this building was completed and opened in 1892. (Naval War College Museum.)

NAVAL WAR COLLEGE AND NAVAL TRAINING STATION, NEWPORT, 1923. Training station drills were frequently held on Dewey Field in front of the college. Here, a recruit formation spells out "Newport." The buildings in the background are, from left to right, the Naval War College, now Luce Hall in the enlarged complex; the Communications Station, built in 1917; and the Naval Training Station administration building, the original home of the college. (Naval War College Museum.)

COLLEGE WITH FIRST ADDITION. This photograph c. 1925 shows the Naval War College with its first Mahan Hall addition, built in 1903. (Naval War College Museum.)

FROM BARRACKS C TO SIMS HALL. This recruit battalion facility of three interconnected buildings called Barracks C was put up in 1904 and remained the property of the Naval Training Station until 1946, when it was taken over by the Naval War College. Its conversion to Sims Hall in 1947 gave the college a facility that became home to the War Gaming Department. This photograph shows the buildings in 1945, during the Second World War. (Naval War College Museum.)

NAVAL WAR COLLEGE CAMPUS. This sketch of an early view of the college campus shows Luce, Mahan, and Pringle Halls, with Sims Hall in the background. (Courtesy Naval War College Foundation.)

ENTRANCE TO MAHAN HALL. A portrait of the college president for whom the building is named appears at the top of the staircase in this 1946 photograph. (Naval War College Museum.)

MAHAN HALL. This photograph by retired Navy Lt. Cmdr. C. Black shows an interior view of Mahan Hall, with a portrait of Alfred Thayer Mahan on the right. Mahan held the rank of captain when he served as Naval War College president from 1886 to 1889 and from 1892 to 1893. (Naval War College Museum.)

Library Reading Room in Mahan Hall. The Mahan Collection is displayed in the bookcase on the right. The Naval War College archivist's office is adjacent to this room. (Naval War College Museum.)

Coasters Harbor Island, Newport, c. 1930. An aerial view of the Naval Training Station shows the Naval War College building on the left; the Communications Station; the college's original home, behind the flagpole; and Quarters AA, the president's residence, dating from 1904. Coddington Point, with various recruit and other station facilities, lies across the water in the background. (Naval War College Museum.)

NAVAL WAR COLLEGE, c. 1930. This view was taken shortly before the addition of Pringle Hall on the left end. (Naval War College Museum.)

PRINGLE HALL AND LUCE HALL, 1963. Pringle Hall (left) was completed in 1934 and named in honor of Rear Adm. Joel Roberts Poinsett Pringle, president of the college from 1927 to 1930. Luce Hall (center), completed in 1892, was the original new construction at the site. (Naval War College Museum.)

ADMIRAL PRINGLE. Rear Adm. Joel Robert Poinsett Pringle served as college president from September 1927 to May 1930. (Naval War College Museum.)

NAVAL WAR COLLEGE, APRIL 3, 1934. This view, looking northeast, shows the west side and south end of the new Pringle Hall addition, adjacent to Luce Hall. (Naval War College Museum.)

LUCE HALL SKYLIGHT. This view, taken on July 6, 1934, shows the new skylight and slate roof on the original college building of 1892. (Naval War College Museum.)

ADMIRAL'S BARGE, NAVAL WAR COLLEGE, C. 1934. This 1930s picture of the Coasters Harbor Island piers shows the Naval War College president's barge, with the training ship *Constellation* in the background. (Naval War College Museum.)

LUCE HALL, 1938. A Naval Training Station pup tent drill is in progress in front of the Naval War College in this picture taken a few years before World War II. (Naval War College Museum.)

COASTERS HARBOR ISLAND IN WARTIME. The Naval War College and Naval Training Station buildings can be seen in the foreground of this photograph taken in March 1944. The sprawling training station barracks and other facilities fill the center portion at Coddington Point. (Naval War College Museum.)

THE NAVY IN NEWPORT, JULY 1944. This wartime photograph shows Coasters Harbor Island with the Naval War College and Naval Training Station, Coddington Point in the near background, and Coddington Cove on the far right. (Courtesy A.S. Nicolosi, Director, Naval War College Museum.)

THE LUCE-MAHAN-PRINGLE COMPLEX, 1953. The Naval War College sits at the edge of Narragansett Bay on Coasters Harbor Island as a ship of the fleet comes down East Passage, heading for open water. (Naval War College Museum.)

SUMMER WHITE HOUSE, NEWPORT, 1957. President Dwight D. Eisenhower and his family occupied this house in "senior officer country" for their month-long residence in Newport. In 1957, 1958, and 1960, the vacationing President also maintained an office as his staff headquarters on the first floor of the original Naval War College building, just down the driveway from the residence. (Naval War College Museum.)

NAVAL WAR COLLEGE, C. 1958. From the flagpole, this photograph catches a seaward view of Luce Hall and Pringle Hall, with just a window bit of Mahan Hall to the rear of Luce Hall. (Naval War College Museum.)

QUARTERS AA. This is a sketch of the residence of the Naval War College president. The building dates from 1904. (Courtesy Naval War College Foundation.)

CAMPUS VIEW, 1968. This 1968 photograph shows Luce Hall and an enlarging campus. (Naval War College Museum.)

Three

Buildings and Facilities II: Further Expansion

In the ensuing late postwar and Cold War period through the 1950s and 1960s, the nominal peacetime politics were reflected in Department of Defense budgets that were increasingly constricted, and the Naval Training Station and naval base of the wartime and immediate postwar periods gave way to a smaller, more inclusive Naval Education and Training Center, which administered numerous school commands.

Recruit training ended in Newport in 1952, and the Naval Training Station was disestablished. A successor command used the original Naval War College building, usually referred to simply as the administration building, as headquarters until 1974. The building also served as headquarters for the Second Naval District, 1902-1919, and for a naval base command established during World War II from 1961. In 1974, both the naval station and naval base were disestablished, replaced by the Naval Education and Training Center, tasked with the support of several school commands in Newport. All of this was propitious, in its way, for the Naval War College, which saw the return of the oldest building on the island to its original command.

With its return to the Naval War College, the building that served as the Newport almshouse from 1820 and that was the first home to the college at its founding in 1884 was named Founders Hall. For two years it was occupied by the Center for Continuing Education and offices of the *Naval War College Review* and of the Naval War College Foundation. In May 1978, after extensive renovation, Founders Hall was dedicated and opened as the Naval War College Museum.

Additions were made to Mahan Hall in 1965 and to Sims Hall in 1968. During his tenure as president, Vice Adm. John T. Hayward had initiated plans for a major new college building program for 1966 through 1968. He sought to provide the Naval War College with new classrooms, administrative offices, a large auditorium, and a new library building. Backed by the college's board of advisors and the chief of naval operations, Adm. Thomas H. Moorer, Hayward energetically sought and obtained support from key members of Congress. Upon Hayward's retirement in 1968, Vice Adm. Richard G. Colbert, the new president of the college, carried the plans forward. He obtained continuing congressional support under difficult conditions and made improvements in the designs of the planned buildings. By arranging to reopen the famous old quarry in Medford, Massachusetts, from which granite facing stone for Pringle Hall was cut in 1933, he ensured that the new buildings would eventually weather to the same color as the older adjacent buildings. Colbert broke ground for the new buildings in a ceremony on the college's 86th anniversary, October 6, 1970. The first segment of the three-part complex, Spruance Hall, was dedicated on December 7, 1971, followed by Conolly Hall on March 28, 1974, and Hewitt Hall on April 28, 1976.

Spruance Hall included the college's largest auditorium facility, which proved useful again and again as various college functions as well as convocations open to the public, such as the evening lecture series sponsored by the Naval War College Foundation, could be presented in a suitable meeting area. Just outside the auditorium, the lobby and wall areas provided a veritable museum space in which to display photographs and artwork of naval and related wartime experiences.

In October 1997, the college held a ground-breaking ceremony for a new Strategic Maritime Research Center. Opened two years later, across a campus street from Hewitt Hall and connected to it by an enclosed overhead walkway, this newest major facility, was named McCarty Little Hall. This three-story building contained a war-gaming facility, administrative offices, and a television studio used to support the war games. Conference rooms, classrooms, and offices to house the Strategic Studies Group and the Decision Support Center were also located in the facility.

The Campus on Narragansett Bay. This spectacular view of the Naval War College takes in the panorama of the Newport Bridge, dedicated June 28, 1969. This longest span in New England provides a roadway link from Newport to Jamestown, on the island, as part of route 138, which connects with interstate routes to Connecticut and New York. (Naval War College Museum.)

NAVAL WAR COLLEGE, C. 1970. This photograph was taken before demolition and removal of the Communications Building between Luce Hall and Founders Hall. Quarters AA can be seen just behind the latter building. (Courtesy R.M. Cembrola, Curator, Naval War College Museum.)

NAVAL WAR COLLEGE. Some years after the 1976 removal of the Communications Building, open space was restored to the area just east of Luce Hall and other buildings were added to the college complex, stretching northward. Both the newly named Founders Hall, the original home of the college from 1884 to 1889, and Quarters AA, the residence of the college president, can be seen on the far right. (Courtesy R.M. Cembrola, Curator, Naval War College Museum.)

College Expansion, 1966–1971. During his tenure as president, Vice Adm. John T. Hayward, in the painting on the left, initiated plans for a major new college building program. He sought to provide the Naval War College with new classrooms, administrative offices, a large auditorium, and a new library building. The president was backed by the college's board of advisors and by Chief of Naval Operations Adm. Thomas H. Moorer. Upon Hayward's retirement in 1968, new president Vice Adm. Richard G. Colbert, on the right, carried the plans forward, obtaining continuing Congressional support and making improvements in building design. (Photograph by the author.)

Spruance Hall. Work on the first buildings of an enlarged Naval War College complex began in the summer of 1970 during the administration of Vice Adm. Richard G. Colbert as president. The view above shows the entrance to Spruance Hall, completed in 1972, and Conolly Hall, built in 1974. Spuance Hall, to the left of the entrance, includes the largest auditorium facility at the college. (Photograph by the author.)

SPRUANCE HALL DEDICATION, 1972. The first building in Adm. John T. Hayward's expansion program was Spruance Hall, named for Adm. Raymond Ames Spruance, Naval War College president from March 1946 to July 1948. Dedication ceremony participants in December 1972 included, from left to right, college president Vice Adm. Stansfield Turner, Mrs. Herman Wouk, Mrs. Spruance, and noted author Herman Wouk. (Naval War College Museum.)

CONSTRUCTION AT THE NAVAL WAR COLLEGE, 1971. Adm. Stansfield Turner, president of the Naval War College, checks the blueprints for Conolly Hall, under construction in the background. With Turner is Capt. Donald Wittschriebe, commanding officer of the Public Works Center. (Naval War College Museum.)

AERIAL PHOTOGRAPH, 1973. Spruance Hall and other buildings of the campus are clearly shown in this photograph, with Conolly Hall under construction in the background on the left. (Naval War College Museum.)

THE NAVY IN NEWPORT, 1975. This aerial photograph taken from the Wanumetonomy Golf & Country Club in Middletown, Rhode Island, in the foreground, shows Navy property in Newport. It provides a panoramic view of the Naval Underwater Systems Center's research and administrative buildings, Navy Piers 1 and 2 in Coddington Cove, Coddington Point, Coasters Harbor Island with the growing Naval War College campus, and the Newport Bridge in the distance—the 15th largest span in the United States when dedicated in 1969. (Official U.S. Navy photograph by R.J. Valentine.)

CONOLLY HALL CONSTRUCTION, 1974. This photograph shows the construction of Conolly Hall under way. (Naval War College Museum.)

CONOLLY HALL CONSTRUCTION. The new building is almost completed in this 1974 scene. (Naval War College Museum.)

CONOLLY HALL DEDICATION. Vice Adm. Stansfield Turner stands at the speaker's podium for the official dedication ceremony for Conolly Hall on March 21, 1974. (Naval War College Museum.)

FOUNDERS HALL, C. 1974. This was the home of the Naval War College when it was founded—a building erected in 1820 by the city of Newport as an asylum for the poor. It was here that the college, the first of its kind in the world, began in 1884, and where Alfred Thayer Mahan wrote his now classic treatise on "The Influence of Sea Power Upon History," published in 1890. The building was designated a National Historic Landmark and placed on the Register of Historic Sites. After renovations, it was dedicated in 1978 as the Naval War College Museum. (Photograph by the author.)

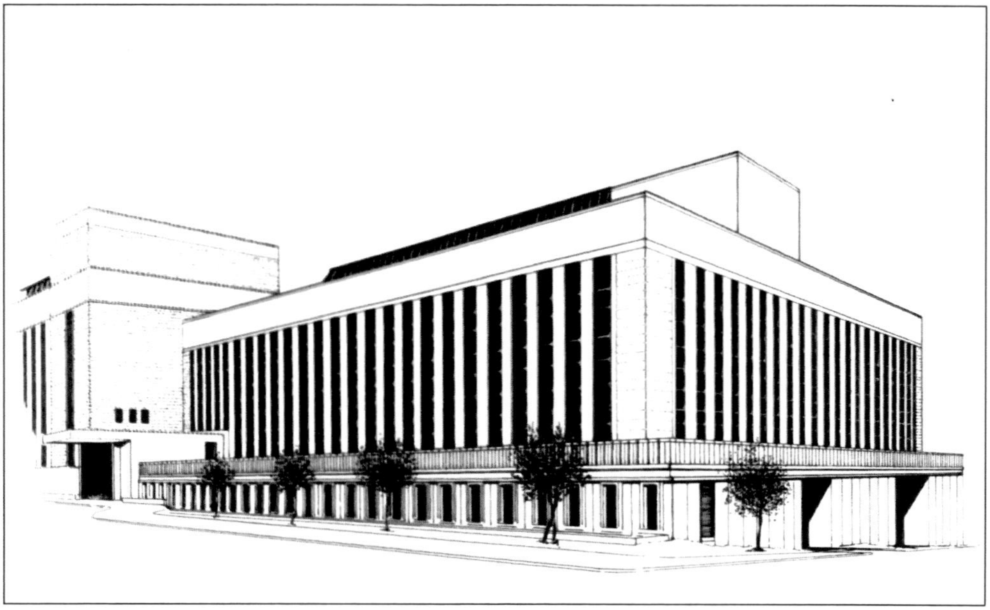

Hewitt Hall, 1976. This artist's sketch from 1976 shows Hewitt Hall. (Naval War College Museum.)

Harry E. Eccles Library, Hewitt Hall. This display is in the foyer of Hewitt Hall, outside the Naval War College library. The library was named for Harry E. Eccles, who devoted much of his Navy career to work in military education. (Photograph by the author.)

RETIRED REAR ADM. HARRY E. ECCLES. With his graduation from the Naval War College in 1943, Harry E. Eccles began a period of nearly four decades of direct, personal involvement in the academic life of the college. Central to his thought was a belief that logistics and leadership are the ways to ultimate success in military operations. All of his personal papers are held in the college archives. As an enduring tribute to his tireless dedication to professional military education, the Naval War College library was named for Eccles on June 10, 1985. (Naval War College Museum.)

THE ECCLES PORTRAIT. Rear Adm. Harry E. Eccles is shown with artist Tony Sarro and Rear Admiral Bates c. 1980. (Naval War College Museum.)

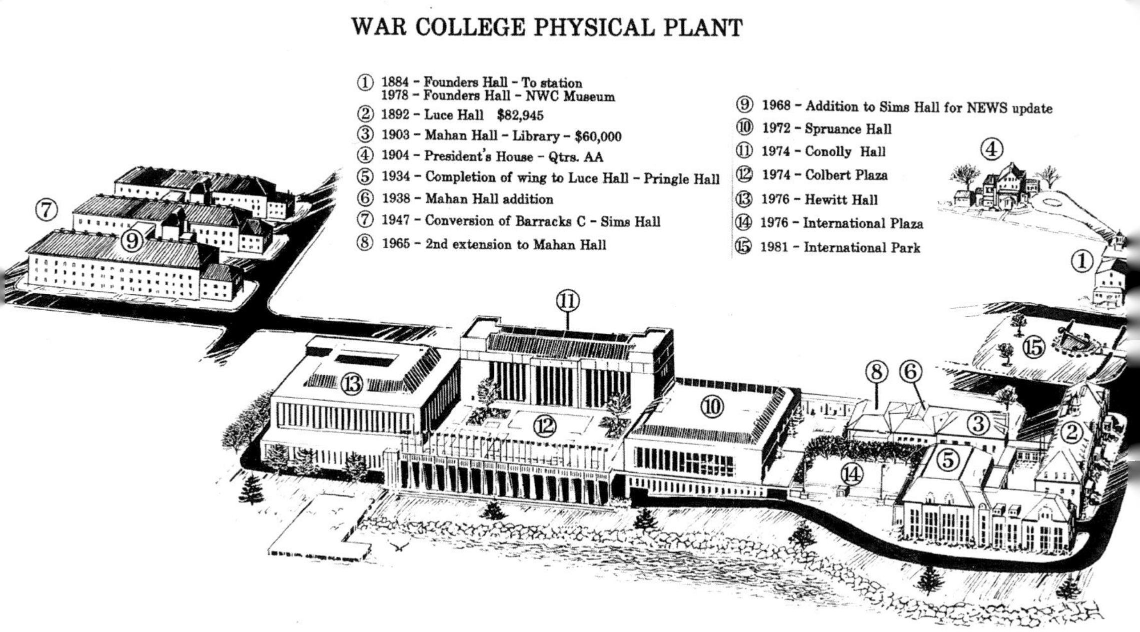

NAVAL WAR COLLEGE BUILDINGS AND CAMPUS, 1981. This sketch gives the layout of the Naval War College physical plant in 1981. The buildings' completion dates and opening dates are included. (Naval War College Museum.)

CAMPUS VIEW. At the nation's oldest service college, naval and military officers of the United States and of the navies of many foreign countries pursue graduate courses in programs designed to prepare them for successfully meeting career responsibilities. (Naval War College Museum.)

'A CENTURY OF EXCELLENCE.' For its 100th anniversary in 1894, the Naval War College issued a philatelic cover in connection with the centennial celebration. The cachet, in oval design, depicts Luce Hall, 1892, the first authorized new construction for the college. A special postmark was available at the designated centennial station in Newport, with a cancellation bearing the Naval War College crest and the words "A Century of Excellence: 1884–1984." (Author's collection.)

MCCARTY LITTLE HALL UNDER CONSTRUCTION. These views show the cross bridge connecting the new building with Hewitt Hall, which includes the Eccles Library, the College Bookstore, and other facilities. (Photographs by the author.)

McCarty Little Hall Opens. The Naval War College and the Naval War College Foundation sponsored the ribbon-cutting ceremony for McCarty Little Hall and the Strategic Maritime Research Center in September 1999. William McCarty Little (1845–1915) was the most important figure in refining the technique of war-gaming so that it could be used as an effective tool to examine and apply the capabilities of rapidly changing naval technology to modern warfare. With Alfred Thayer Mahan and Stephen B. Luce, McCarty Little made one of the most prominent and most enduring contributions in the history of the Naval War College. In 1910, Luce wrote that through McCarty Little's ingenuity and indefatigable work, "the naval war game became a recognized part of the college curriculum. His work has contributed very largely to whatever success the college has achieved." McCarty Little entered the U.S. Naval Academy when it was located in Newport during the Civil War and graduated in 1866. He served with Luce in succeeding years, including as executive officer of Luce's flagship as commander, apprentice training squadron. After retirement McCarty Little served as a volunteer staff member when the Naval War College opened in 1884 and he established the college's first library. In 1903, Congress assigned him permanently to active duty on the retired list with the faculty of the college. (Naval War College Foundation.)

QUARTERS A. In the spring of 1999 when this photograph was taken, Quarters A was the residence of college provost Rear Adm. P.A.C. Long and Mrs. Long. This building was used as a residence and summer White House by Gen. Dwight D. Eisenhower in the late 1950s and 1960 for his monthly stay in Newport when he was President of the United States. (Photograph by the author.)

QUARTERS AA. At the time this photograph was taken, Quarters AA was the residence of Naval War College president Vice Adm. Arthur K Cebrowski. PH3 (SW) Stephanie Allison captured this springtime scene in "senior officer country" with a digital camera. (Courtesy of the photographer.)

Four

COURSES, CURRICULUM, AND CONVOCATIONS

Like all academic institutions, the Naval War College has had curriculum changes and additions throughout its history. In its early days, the college offered courses in war planning and weapons evaluation and for a decade was consolidated with the pioneer Naval Torpedo Station. That consolidation was revoked in 1898. In 1893 the "main problem" was added to the curriculum, with sections preparing monographs and drawing up war charts and defense plans. War-gaming was a part of the curriculum of the college since 1886 and, as such, the college is the oldest war-gaming facility in the United States. More than 100 years after the inauguration of that curricular innovation, a specially equipped building, McCarty Little Hall, was authorized in 1996 for war-gaming.

As the college's first president, Commodore Stephen Luce established the Naval War College as "a place of original research on all questions relating to war, and to statesmanship connected to war or the prevention of war." In setting up a curriculum of "lectures, readings, and seminars," the first president set a course for the college which endures to this day.

In recruiting talented naval officers, as well as officers from other services and civilian scholars, Luce also set a precedent that is still the hallmark of the college's unique curriculum and faculty programs. He saw that a study of strategy, tactics, and operations upon a core of history were the natural way for the college to go.

By 1911, the long course was begun, with diplomas given out; and in 1913, the thesis came into use. A correspondence course was inaugurated the following year. Beginning in 1919, the staff organization included the departments of Command, Strategy, Tactics, Correspondence, and Administration. Both junior and senior courses were established in 1923, the junior course being the forerunner of the later command and staff course. In 1931, a research department was established for war games. In 1940, both junior and senior courses were 11 months in length but in 1941, the exigencies of the time saw the change to five months duration for both. In the immediate postwar period, a separate logistics course was begun in 1947, and in 1948 the *Publication for Information Source* for officers was introduced, which became the *Naval War College Review* in 1952. An advanced course in study in strategy and sea power began in 1951 and was discontinued in 1957. In 1954, a two- year course in naval warfare was introduced. The naval command course was established in 1956. As the 1960s emerged, the first Annual Naval Reserve Officers School Instructor Seminar was held at the college, the correspondence course department became the extension education department, and, as world developments seemed to suggest the need, a counterinsurgency course was introduced into the overall curriculum. The Naval Command College, now called the Naval Staff College, was established with its own specialized curriculum to train naval officers from friendly foreign nations.

During his tenure as president, 1977–1979, Adm. James B Stockdale introduced and taught a course entitled "The Foundations of Moral Obligations." In 1998, Class 53 of the Naval Staff College was the first of the foreign officer training class to have a woman officer aboard. She was also the first naval officer to attend from New Zealand.

At present, the Naval War College consists of the resident schools, a Center for Continuing Education, and a Center for Naval Warfare Studies for advanced research on current naval questions. The college is fully accredited by the New England Association of Schools and Colleges to offer the master's degree. Graduates of the correspondence course program and foreign students in that and other programs receive diplomas issued by the college.

NAVAL TACTICS LECTURE, 1888. Officer students listen to a lecture in naval tactics in the original building of the Naval War College on Coasters Harbor Island, Newport. (Naval War College Museum.)

CLASS IN WAR GAMING, 1914. An 1866 graduate of the Naval Academy at Annapolis, William McCarty Little explored the war-gaming ideas that Vice Adm. P.H. Colomb and Fred T. Jane had developed in Britain, and introduced war-gaming into the U.S. Navy. In 1886, McCarty Little gave the first formal lecture on war-gaming and for nearly 30 years continued to lecture and to develop its methodology. He was an active member of the Naval War College faculty from 1903 to 1915. (Naval War College Museum.)

CLASS OF 1920. This October 1919 photograph shows Rear Adm. William Snowden Sims, president of the college, in the front center with the staff and the Class of 1920, which graduated in May 1920. The photographer was T.H. Owens. (Naval War College Museum.)

CLASS OF 1923. Cmdr. Chester W. Nimitz, future admiral and World War II commander in chief in the Pacific, appears in this class picture in the top row, seventh from the right. (Naval War College Museum.)

President Spruance. Adm. Raymond A. Spruance served as college president from March 1946 to June 1948. At the end of World War II, he was named commander in chief in the Pacific, replacing Chester Nimitz, who became chief of naval operations. Spruance served in his new position only ten months before joining the Naval War College as its president on March 1, 1946. It is said that Spruance elected to go to Newport because he always considered the college presidency as one of the most important jobs in the Navy. He knew Newport from personal experience; he graduated from the college's senior course in 1927 and served two separate times on the staff in the next decade. During his tenure as president, he revitalized the college from the short-course specialized training facility it had become during the war and introduced a new and challenging curriculum. (Photograph courtesy Naval War College Public Affairs Office.)

Admiral Spruance at Marine Review. This photograph, c. 1948, shows Adm. Raymond A. Spruance at a review of the Marines detachment. (Naval War College Museum.)

WAR-GAMING CLASS. This undated photograph, perhaps *c.* 1950, shows Naval War College students participating in a war-gaming exercise in Pringle Hall. (Naval War College Museum.)

INTERNATIONAL LAW STUDY GROUP. An international law study group is shown at the Naval War College in 1961. (Naval War College Museum.)

Naval Command Course No.1, 1956. Students attending the Naval War College naval command course for foreign officers were given a tour of Washington, D.C. The tour included a visit to the White House on September 7, 1956. (Naval War College Museum.)

Visit to Washington. Students and staff of the first naval command course are shown on the steps of the Capitol on September 8, 1956, during their visit to Washington, D.C. Capt. Richard G. Colbert, director of the course, stands in the back row, second from the right. (Official U.S. Navy photograph.)

Naval Warfare Course for Reservists. Five Naval Reserve Officers from the First Naval District attending a special two-week naval warfare course posed for this group picture outside Luce Hall. They were part of a group of 100 senior reservists from throughout the country attending the special course for U.S. Navy, Marine, and Coast Guard reserve officers June 4-15, 1962, at the Naval War College. The officers, from left to right, are Cmdr. T.H. Goodgame, Andover, Massachusetts; Cmdr. F.E. Shaw, Nashua, New Hampshire; Cmdr. R.G. King, Winchester, Massachusetts; Capt. R.T. Rounds, Hyannis, Massachusetts; and Cmdr. P.H. Winder, Lexington, Massachusetts. (Naval War College Museum.)

Naval Aviators at Summer Course. These naval aviators were among reservists attending the naval warfare course at Newport in the summer of 1962. (Naval War College Museum.)

PROFESSORS ATTEND RESERVE COURSE IN NEWPORT. Capt. Everett T. Curry, left, and Cmdr. Charles L. Smith attended the two-week Reserve Course at the Naval War College in June 1962. Both attendees were college professors—Capt. Curry at the University of Illinois and Capt. Smith at Drake University—and both were the only specialists of their kind (Curry in the Medical Service Corps and Smith a chaplin) in the group pf 100 senior reserve officers of the U.S. Navy, Marine Corps, and Coast Guard taking the active duty training in Newport. (Naval War College Museum.)

AVERILL HARRIMAN ADDRESS, 1962. W. Averill Harriman, assistant secretary of state for Far Eastern affairs, is escorted to Pringle Auditorium at the Naval War College by Vice Adm. Bernard L. Austin, president. Mr. Harriman, governor of New York from 1954 to 1958 and a former secretary of commerce, addressed the staff and students of the college on November 7, 1962, speaking on "U.S. Objectives, Programs and Prospects in Asia and the Western Pacific." Behind Harriman and Austin is Amb. Roy R. Rubottom, State Department advisor at the College. (Naval War College Museum.)

Dedication of New Academic Chair. Attendees at the dedication ceremony of the Milton E. Miles Chair of International Relations at the Naval War College on June 27, 1962, included Vice Adm. Bernard L. Austin, third from left, president of the college; and Wilma Miles, second from right, the widow of Vice Adm. Milton E. Miles, the honoree for whom the chair was established. (Naval War College Museum.)

Miles Chair Dedication. On hand for the dedication ceremony were, from left to right, Mrs. August Miller, wife of the chair holder; Wilma Miles, widow of Vice Adm. Milton E. Miles, the honoree; and Vice Adm. Bernard L. Austin, college president. A photograph of Miles is on the wall. (Naval War College Museum.)

French Ambassador Hervé Alphand Speaks on France. Leaving to return to Washington, D.C., His Excellency Hervé Alphand, left, French ambassador to the United States, and Madame Alphand, third from left, bid good-bye to Vice Adm. Bernard L. Austin, Naval War College president, and Mrs. Austin at the admiral's quarters. Alphand addressed the staff and students of the college on November 13, 1962, speaking on "France: Problems and Prospects." (Naval War College Museum.)

Raytheon President Lectures. Charles F. Adams, president of Raytheon Company, is escorted by college president Vice Adm. Bernard L. Austin to Pringle Auditorium. There, Adams addressed the staff and students on November 20, 1962. His topic was "Science and Technology in Strategy." (Naval War College Museum.)

BRITISH AMBASSADOR DAVID ORMSBY GORE, 1963. The British ambassador to the United States received an honor guard salute on his arrival at the Naval War College to address the staff and students on November 15, 1963. Sir David Ormsby Gore, who was invested Knight Commander of the Order of St. Michael and St. George by Her Majesty the Queen just before sailing for his post in Washington, D.C., in October 1961, lectured on "Great Britain: Problems and Prospects." Gore discussed current political, economic, and military developments and trends within Great Britain, and gave a personal analysis of their subsequent impact on the future position of Great Britain in the contemporary world. (Naval War College Museum.)

ADLAI STEVENSON AT GLOBAL STRATEGY DISCUSSION. Ambassador Adlai Stevenson enters the Naval War College to give an address at the Global Strategy Discussion in 1963. With him is Capt. Richard Ironmonger (SC) of the Naval War College staff, escort officer for Stevenson. (Naval War College Museum.)

Rear Admiral Hyland Speaks on Strategy. Rear Adm. John J. Hyland, right, spoke on "Naval Implications of Reconnaissance Satellites" on January 30, 1964. The talk by Hyland, who was assistant director of the Strategic Plans Division office, chief of naval operations, included the effects upon the strategic and tactical employment of naval forces which could result from the anticipated reconnaissance satellite of the predictable future. (Naval War College Museum.)

Felix De Weldon Speaks at Change of Command. Internationally prominent sculptor and Newport friend of the college Felix de Weldon addresses the convocation at the change of command ceremony for outgoing president Vice Adm. Bernard L. Austin, third from right, and new president Vice Adm. Charles L. Melson, second from right. (Naval War College Museum.)

CHANGE OF COMMAND, 1964. Retiring college president Vice Adm. Bernard L. Austin and his replacement Vice Adm. Charles L. Melson exchange salutes. The ceremony was held outside Luce Hall. (Naval War College Museum.)

FOREIGN OFFICERS AT THE NAVAL COMMAND COLLEGE. This picture, taken January 12, 1966, shows three foreign officers of the student body: Cmdr. John H. G. Bovey, Royal Canadian Navy; Cmdr. Sheikh A. Rauf, Pakistan Navy; and Cmdr. Bruce H. Loyton, Royal Australian Navy. (Naval War College Museum.)

NAVAL COMMAND COLLEGE, CLASS OF 1968. This photograph shows the Class of 1968 of the Naval Command College. (Naval War College Museum.)

STUDENTS VISIT NASA, 1968. Members of the Naval Command College visit the Manned Spacecraft Center in Houston, Texas. (Naval War College Museum.)

Director of the Correspondence School, 1970. Marine Col. Arthur Nelson Jr. pores over lesson material in his office at the Naval War College. (Official U.S. Navy photograph by PHC W.M. Powers, Naval War College Public Affairs Office.)

Lesson Evaluation. Lt. Cmdr. Peter Ogle of the Correspondence School faculty evaluates a lesson installment sent by a student taking the command logistics course. (Official U.S. Navy photograph by PHC W.M. Powers, Naval War College Public Affairs Office.)

CURRICULUM REVISIONS. Cmdr. Edwin E. Hanson, left, and Capt. Elizabeth S. Garrison of the Correspondence School discuss proposed changes for update of school curriculum in this May 1970 photograph. Courses are periodically revised to reflect the introduction of new tactics and strategy into the Navy. (Official U.S. Navy photograph by PHC W.M. Powers, Naval War College Public Affairs Office.)

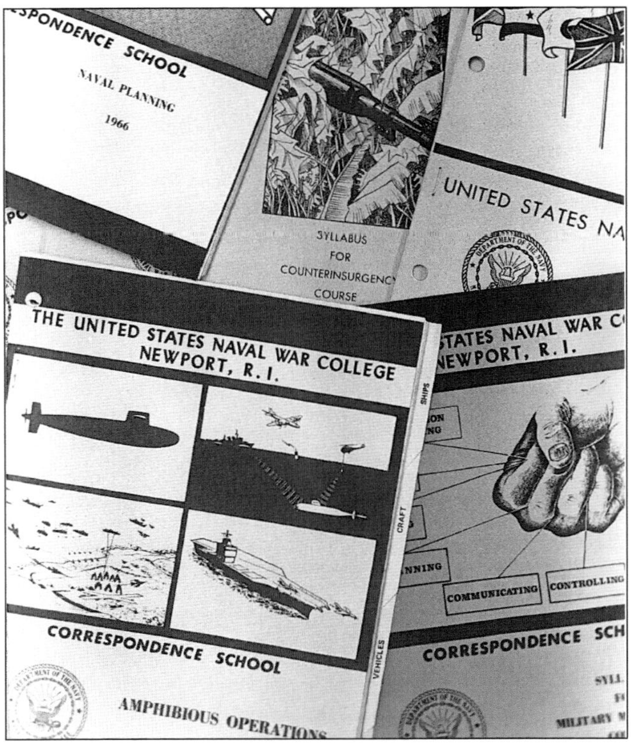

LESSON BOOKS. This photograph shows some of the lesson books available from the Correspondence School of the Naval War College in Newport. (Official U.S. Navy photograph by PHC W.M. Powers, Naval War College Public Affairs Office.)

CONFERENCE OF THE AMERICAS, 1971. The front of the Naval War College is flanked with the flags of member countries attending the annual conference in Newport. (Naval War College Museum.)

THE NAVAL WAR COLLEGE'S COLLEGE OF NAVAL COMMAND STAFF AND STUDENTS. Officers attending the course appear in a classroom photograph taken September 6, 1973. (Naval War College Museum.)

CONVOCATION, 1973. College president Vice Adm. Stansfield Turner (at podium) presides at the 1973 convocation. Seated to the right of Turner is Secretary of the Navy William J. Middendorf. (Naval War College Museum.)

Secretary Schlesinger Arrives to Address College. Secretary of Defense James R. Schlesinger talks with Vice Adm. Julien J. LeBourgeois, Naval War College president at the Naval Education and Training Center in Newport on May 30, 1975. Schlesinger gave a classified address to the U.S. students as part of the annual program of having top Defense Department civilian and military leaders lecture at the college. In the background is Bing West, special assistant to the defense secretary and former member of the Naval War College faculty. (Official U.S. Navy photograph by PHC Ralph Payne, courtesy Naval War College Museum.)

Schlesinger Visit, 1975. Defense Secretary James R. Schlesinger talks with Naval War College president Vice Adm. Julien J. LeBourgeois as they walk from the helicopter pad to where the secretary is to give a classified presentation to the college's U.S. students. (Naval War College Museum.)

NAVY SECRETARY MIDDENDORF IN NEWPORT. In the mid-1970s, Secretary of the Navy William J. Middendorf was at the Naval War College for a ribbon-cutting ceremony for the opening of the Center for Advanced Research. (Naval War College Museum.)

NASH MEMORIAL AWARD LECTURE, 1976. Dean Rusk, secretary of state during the Kennedy and Johnson administrations, reviewed international relations in the nuclear era in his Frank C. Nash Memorial Award Lecture at the Naval War College on April 12, 1976. (Naval War College Museum.)

Naval Command Course Founder Speaks at 20th Anniversary. The celebrated naval commander Adm. Arleigh Burke distinguished himself in World War II in 22 surface actions in the Solomons, where he won his nickname "Thirty-One Knot Burke." He was chief of naval operations for an unprecedented six years, from 1955 to 1961, a period in which the *Polaris* ballistic missile submarine program was developed. His experience in Allied and NATO operations led him to found the first international program at the Naval War College—the Naval Command Course, later the Naval Command College—which first convened in 1956. On July 13, 1976, he spoke at the dedication of International Plaza between Spruance, Mahan, and Pringle Halls, in commemoration of the 20th anniversary of the Naval Command Course. (Courtesy *Naval War College Review*.)

Secretary of the Navy Lehman. Conferees of the Current Strategy Forum in 1983 hear an address by Navy Secretary John Lehman in Spruance Auditorium. The forum is one of a number of major conferences held at the college each year. (Naval War College Museum.)

EXTRACURRICULAR: STAFF AND STUDENT FLOWER SHOW. Naval War College staff and students participated in this flower show held in June 1977 in the lobby of Spruance Hall. Many other activities involving wives and families occur throughout the year. (Official U.S. Navy photograph by W.J. Arnold.)

NAVAL STAFF COLLEGE. A class of the Naval Staff College stands for a group picture. Begun in 1972, the Naval Staff College is one of four resident colleges of the Naval War College, its mid-grade officers drawn from specific countries invited by the chief of naval operations. Its mission is to assist the highly selected international students in developing professional and managerial skills to prepare them for more senior positions in their home navies. Taught in English by Naval War College faculty, the five-and-one-half-month course emphasizes naval planning and decision making. An important part of the curriculum is the information program visits made throughout the United States to provide students with a balanced understanding of society, institutions, and culture. (Naval War College Public Affairs Office.)

President Stockdale in Class. During his presidency of the college from 1977 to 1979, Vice Adm. James B. Stockdale added a course in military ethics as part of the traditional triad of studies in strategy, management, and operations. In teaching the elective course called "The Foundations of Moral Obligations," Stockdale took his class of some 100 students deep into the philosophies of Aristotle, Plato, Epictus, and Kant, as well as of later authors such as Emerson, Lenin, Dostoyevski, and Solzhenitsyn. (Courtesy *All Hands* and the Naval War College Museum.)

NEW ENDOWED CHAIR, 1998. The Capt. Jerome Eli Levy Chair of Economic Geography and National Security is funded by an endowment to the Naval War College Foundation provided by Levy, the chair's namesake. Professor Andrew L. Ross was named the first chair holder. Levy, a native of New York, enlisted in the Navy's V-7 program in 1942. He became a captain in the Naval Reserve in 1967. He is a trustee and life member of the foundation. The photograph taken at the members meeting in June 1998 shows, from left to right, Rear Adm. James R. Stark, former president of the college; Capt. Robert Turpin, chairman of the foundation; Levy; and Adm. Jay Johnson, chief of naval operations. (Naval War College Foundation.)

A FIRST FOR THE NAVAL STAFF COLLEGE. Class 53 welcomed Lt. Cmdr. Maxime Lawes as the first-ever female officer to attend the Naval Staff College. Lawes was also the first New Zealander at the college. Commissioned from the "deck," or enlisted ranks, she was at the time of her joining the class a supply officer in the Royal New Zealand Navy. She participated in the first trial at sea for women in her service, was the first naval woman officer to be assigned as aide-de-camp for the New Zealand governor general, and was the first woman trained as a flight deck officer of a warship. Among other credits of her tenure in Newport, Lawes was elected president of her class. (Naval War College Foundation.)

Director, Naval Staff College. Named to head the Naval Staff College in 1998, Capt. James R. Stapleford, previously served as the naval attaché and attaché for air at the U.S. Embassy in Ottawa. He earlier served as chief of nuclear strategic plans at the Pacific command in Hawaii and graduated from the Foreign Service Institute language and area studies program. (Naval War College Foundation.)

'TR's Navy' Exhibit. Since its opening in the 1970s, the Naval War College Museum has served as an important resource on naval history, providing support to the college, its staff, and its students. The museum's exhibits and displays cover a wide range of subjects from the local naval history of Narragansett Bay to the science and technology of torpedoes, PT boats, and war-gaming. Pictured here is a scale model of the Panana Canal, part of the exhibit "TR's Navy," which highlights the influence of Theodore Roosevelt on naval planning and the U.S. Navy in the United States, Hawaii, Panama, and elsewhere. The museum's extensive photograph files provide researchers with coverage of virtually all subjects connected with the college, from the physical plant to the staff, guest speakers, convocations, and other functions. Ongoing displays feature scale models of historic vessels, such as the *Constitution*, British HMS *Victory*, and the 20-gun brig *Niagara* in which Commodore Oliver Hazard Perry won the Battle of Lake Erie on September 13, 1813. (Naval War College Museum.)

Five

CELEBRITIES AND MORE: A SAMPLE OF NOTABLE VISITORS

The very nature of the Naval War College makes it a place for guest visitors and speakers, many of whom are well-known political figures or representatives of the U.S. civilian and military defense establishment. From time to time, other visitors both foreign and domestic come to Newport for a wide range of reasons: governmental, diplomatic, or personal. As at other colleges, graduations and convocations bring noted speakers to participate in the ceremonies. In addition, a number of Naval War College guests from all walks of life speak at the Contemporary Lecture Series, present the Frank C. Nash Memorial Award Lecture, or deliver other presentations throughout a given year.

As a result, the Naval War College staff and students experience a considerably wider range and depth of outside personalities, opinions, and viewpoints than might ordinarily be found at the more traditional public or private college and university. Both U. S. students and those attending the international programs profit by being exposed to various aspects of U.S. society, culture, and institutions. The many subjects that speakers discuss range from the purely military to types of government, economics, politics, global concerns, and modern science and technology that affects decision making.

Many of the celebrities pictured in this chapter tie in with the Naval War College academic program. Other notable figures who have come to the campus can be found elsewhere in the book. Chapter Four in particular includes a number of special lecturers and other speakers at dedications or convocations, which serve as a regular part of the college's academic program or are closely related to it. Visiting speakers have included Raytheon Company's president Charles F. Adams, French Ambassador Hervé Alphand, British Ambassador Sir David Ormsby Gore, Secretary of the Navy John Lehman, Secretary of the Navy William J. Middendorf, Secretary of State Dean Rusk, Secretary of Defense James R. Schlesinger, and sculptor Felix de Welden. Other visiting government officials, such as Theodore Roosevelt, both as assistant secretary of the Navy and as president of the United States, and Secretary of the Navy Josephus Daniels may be found among the photographs in Chapter One.

The sample of visitors here is presented in roughly alphabetical order, with captions giving the date in Newport and an indication of the reason for the person's visit to the Naval War College campus.

WILLIAM BUCKLEY, 1973. Distinguished author, magazine editor, and television commentator on political matters, William F. Buckley is shown at the podium in Spruance Auditorium during a lecture at the Naval War College. (Naval War College Museum.)

PRINCE ANDREW, 1983. Prince Andrew of Great Britain stopped by the Naval War College Museum on a visit in 1983. He is shown with his Royal Navy aide looking at books on display at the museum store and with Dr. John Hattendorf, left, professor of history at the Naval War College. (Naval War College Museum.)

JIMMY CARTER, 1973. Vice Adm. Stansfield Turner, Naval War College president, greets visiting Georgia Gov. Jimmy Carter in June 1973. When Carter later became President of the United States, he appointed Turner director of the Central Intelligence Agency. (Naval War College Museum.)

GEN. MARK CLARK AND ADM. HENRY HEWITT, 1964. Prior to addressing the Naval War College students on February 14, 1964, retired army Gen. Mark W. Clark, center, meets retired Navy Adm. Henry K. Hewitt, right, the naval commander who landed the general and his allied troops at Salerno, Italy, in World War II. The meeting took place in the office of Vice Adm. Bernard L. Austin, left, president of the college. Clark's army career spanned two world wars. At the time of his Newport visit, he was president of the Citadel, the military college of South Carolina in Charleston. Hewitt, temporarily in Newport, met Clark and heard him speak on "Leadership and the Military Commander." (Naval War College Museum.)

EISENHOWER, 1957. Rear Adm. Henry Cromelin, left, of the Newport Naval Base escorts Pres. Dwight D. Eisenhower to a helicopter about to depart for Quonset Point Naval Air Station. Eisenhower is accompanied by naval aide Capt. E.D. Durand. (Atlantic Fleet Camera Party photograph, courtesy Naval War College Archives and Dwight D. Eisenhower Library.)

JOHN KENNETH GALBRAITH, 1979. John Kenneth Galbraith, noted economist, author, and former ambassador to India from 1961 to 1963, is shown during a 1979 address to the Naval War College. (Naval War College Museum.)

JOHN GLENN, C. 1978. Astronaut and U.S. Congressman John Glenn strolls on the Naval War College campus during a visit with his friend Vice Adm. James B. Stockdale, president of the college. (Courtesy *All Hands* and the Naval War College Museum.)

GENERAL GRISWOLD, 1961. Air Force Gen. F.H. Griswold, National War College commandant, visited the Naval War College on November 8, 1961. Shown, from left to right, are General Griswold; Rear Adm. R.H. Phillips, deputy commandant, National War College; Rear Adm. A.M. Jackson, chief of staff, Naval War College; and Capt. T.D. Cunningham, head of the college's academic plans department. (Naval War College Museum.)

General Hamlett, 1963. Gen. Barksdale Hamlett, vice chief of staff of the U.S. Army, gave a lecture on December 17, 1963, to the students and staff of the Naval War College. He spoke on the then current U.S. Army capabilities in counterinsurgency as viewed on a worldwide basis. Hamlett was an artillery officer and served in the European theater of operations in World War II. He attended Ecole de Guerre in France and the National War College, and he was U.S. commander in Berlin from June 1957 to December 1959. He is shown above with War College president Vice Adm. Bernard L. Austin. (Naval War College Museum.)

Averill Harriman, 1963. W. Averill Harriman, then undersecretary of state for political affairs, spoke on "The Role of the Department of State in National Security" at the Naval War College on August 30, 1963. (Naval War College Museum.)

Fleet Admiral Sir Casper John, 1963. The British Royal Navy visitor greets area flag officers and Naval War College staff officers during a visit to the college on May 27, 1963. (Naval War College Museum.)

Salute to the Fleet Admiral. Sir Casper John, first sea lord and chief of naval staff, Great Britain, foreground, takes a 19-gun salute. John's visit to the Naval War College included an address to the staff and students. Rear Adm. A.H. Taylor, base commander, and Rear Adm. R.D. Bogle, War College chief of staff, render salutes. (Naval War College Museum.)

President John F. Kennedy, 1961. The President of the United States arrives at the Naval War College in September 1961 for a news briefing on his new appointee as director of the Central Intelligence Agency. With the President are Allen W. Dulles, the then current director, and John A. McCone, who was to succeed him. (Naval War College Museum.)

Kennedy, Dulles, and McCone. Naval War College president Vice Adm. Bernard L. Austin accompanies Pres. John F. Kennedy to Pringle Hall for the news briefing. With the President are Allen W. Dulles, CIA director, and his replacement John A. McCone. (Naval War College Museum.)

HENRY KISSINGER, 1978. Contemporary Lecture Series speaker Henry Kissinger, former secretary of state, is on stage in Spruance Auditorium on March 8, 1978. The Contemporary Lecture Series is sponsored by the Naval War College Foundation and features distinguished leaders of all walks of life. It is an evening affair, open to the general public. (Naval War College Museum.)

AMBASSADOR LODGE, 1961. Henry Cabot Lodge, ambassador to the United Nations, is shown with Naval War College president Vice Adm. Bernard L. Austin in September 1961. (Naval War College Museum.)

NIMITZ AND EISENHOWER, 1960. Retired Fleet Admiral Chester W. Nimitz, is in discussion at the Naval War College with vacationing President Dwight D. Eisenhower and college president Vice Adm. Bernard L. Austin. During World War II, Nimitz was commander of U.S. Naval Forces in the Pacific, from 1941 to 1945. Following the war he served as chief of naval operations. (Naval War College Museum.)

CLAIBORNE PELL. Rhode Island Sen. Claiborne Pell, a resident of Newport, took the opportunity to visit the Naval War College from time to time. He is shown here with college president Vice Adm. Bernard L. Austin in the early 1960s. (Naval War College Museum.)

Marshal Pétain, 1931. Marshal Henri Pétain and other distinguished French visitors came to Newport in 1931. They arrived on the French cruisers *Duquesne* and *Suffren* and were accompanied by U.S. Army Gen. John J. Pershing. In later years Pétain lost considerable repute through his affiliation with the Vichy government during the German occupation of France in the 1940s. This photograph taken on October 27, 1931, shows an exhibition drill of apprentice seamen of the Naval Training Station. The Navy training ship the USS *Constellation* is offshore to the right. (Naval War College Museum.)

Pétain at Newport. Henri Phillippe Pétain, marshal of France, along with a French delegation, visited the Naval War College in the early 1930s. Army Gen. John J. Pershing is also shown in the photograph, second from left on the stairs. (Naval War College Museum.)

KATE SMITH, 1943. The popular singer came to Newport as a USO performer during World War II. Shown with her are Rear Adm. William S. Pye, president of the Naval War College, and Capt. C.W. McGrudder, commanding officer of the Naval Station. (Naval War College Museum.)

CARDINAL SPELLMAN. This scene in Mahan Library shows New York's Francis Cardinal Spellman on a visit in the early 1960s. (Naval War College Museum.)

Herman Wouk, 1980. Noted author Herman Wouk spoke to staff and students at the Naval War College on April 18, 1980. During his visit, he stopped by the Mahan Library. (Naval War College Museum.)

Major Yates, February 4, 1964. College president Vice Adm. Bernard L. Austin accepts a letter written by Naval War College founder Stephen B. Luce from army Maj. Joseph J. Yates Jr., great-grandnephew of Luce, the college's first president. (Naval War College Museum.).

Six

The Naval War College Museum

An article that appeared in *Foundation Notes* on the 20th anniversary of the Naval War College Museum stated the following: "The two decades in historic Founders Hall, the stately white stone building on the southern perimeter of the campus, has seen the activity progress from a modest one-floor exhibit and ad hoc displays on the college and Navy in Newport, to the current large space of two floors with a total of six galleries (each 1,300 square feet) containing both permanent exhibits on the history of naval installations in the region and special exhibits (four to six months duration) on naval warfare and naval regional history."

The present one-site Naval War College Museum was established in the 1970s, but the building it occupies has a history dating back to the early days of Newport. Completed in 1820 on Coasters Harbor Island as the Newport Asylum for the Poor, the building served in its capacity as a refuge for the poor until 1881, when the Navy purchased the property. In 1883, the island became the site of the Newport Naval Training Station, the first shore-based recruit training station in America. A year later, the building itself became home to the newly established Naval War College.

The original building became Naval Training Station property in 1889 and served both that command and others as an administration building until 1974, when it again became Naval War College property and was named and dedicated as Founders Hall. Three years later the first floor was renovated for use as a museum and in May 1978, the Naval War College Museum was dedicated and opened to the public.

Previously, museum pieces had been located variously throughout the campus buildings—Luce Hall, Mahan Hall, and Sims Hall—and as the new construction of the 1970s was completed, Spruance Hall, Conolly Hall, and Hewitt Hall also offered displays. With the May 1978 dedication, the Naval War College Museum became a separate and distinct building, and its basic theme was the history of naval warfare and the naval heritage of Narragansett Bay. After several years of using only the first floor for museum space, the entire building became available for museum purposes in 1983. As a result, further renovation was undertaken which doubled the exhibit space. When the renovated building with its newly enlarged exhibit space was ready, the Naval War College Museum reopened on October 6, 1984, the college's 100th anniversary.

Museum record files and administrative offices for the director, curator, and staff are located on the third-floor and basement levels. The galleries with exhibits both permanent and special are on the first and second floors. Today, a museum store is operated by the Naval War College Foundation on the first floor across from the main visitor entrance, and the museum has a student internship program with area colleges that provides valuable assistance in record keeping, file maintenance, and a number of other museum functions. Open to the public, the Naval War College Museum proudly contributes not only to the college's educational mission but also to the knowledge of visitors who come throughout the year.

NAVAL WAR COLLEGE MUSEUM, 1981. The Naval War College in 1974 celebrated the return of its first home, long used for administrative purposes by the Naval Training Station and other training commands. It was named Founders Hall, and plans were made for making the building the site of a college museum. In May 1978, the museum opened on the first floor, featuring exhibits on the founding and early years of the college and the naval heritage of Narragansett Bay. Additional renovations took place during between 1983 and 1984, and the museum opened in November 1984 with exhibits on its two main floors, administrative offices, and a finished basement and a rear annex with elevator and stairways. (Naval War College Museum.)

OPENING OF THE MUSEUM, 1978. Attending the ribbon-cutting ceremony for the opening of the newly dedicated Naval War College Museum are John Monsarrat, Naval War College Foundation president; Felix deWelden, guest speaker; Anthony Nicolosi, museum director; and Captain Platt, deputy to the president of the Naval War College. (Naval War College Museum.)

NATIONAL HISTORIC LANDMARK. The original building of the Naval War College, which became home to the Naval War College Museum in the 1970s, was declared a registered National Historic Landmark in 1965. This stone marker is located just outside the front entrance of the building. (Photograph by the author.)

'Founding and Early Years.' This exhibit, 1978-1983, was located on the first floor of the building and was the first of the newly opened museum's offerings. (Naval War College Museum.)

Classroom of 1888. One of the displays in the first exhibit shows a 1888 classroom scene with an instructor and students in the original building. (Naval War College Museum.)

Marine Corps Exhibit Opening, 1979. Interested visitors settle on the lawn in front of the Naval War College Museum to watch the ceremony for the opening of an exhibit on the U.S. Marine Corps in Newport. (Naval War College Museum.)

Conolly Exhibit, 1980. Part of the "Founding and Early Years" exhibit, this display features photographs, medals, and other material concerning Richard L. Conolly, president of the Naval War College from December 1950 to November 1953. Conolly Hall (see pp. 50 ff.) was named for him. (Naval War College Museum.)

Display Panel. This display centers on torpedo boats and is part of another early exhibit. (Naval War College Museum.)

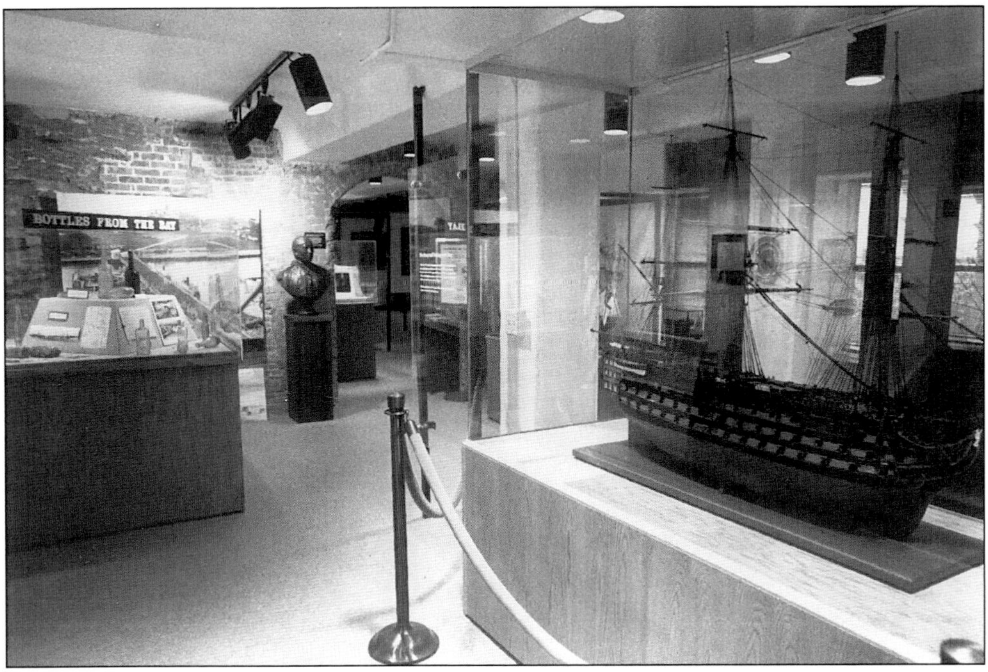

Center Gallery Exhibit. "Bottles in the Bay," featuring glass bottles retrieved from Narragansett Bay, was the basis for this display in the museum. In the right forefront is a model of the *Constitution*, which had a historic role in the early history of Newport and Coasters Harbor Island. (Naval War College Museum.)

EXHIBIT ON WAR-GAMING. This photograph of August 1986 shows a display on the museum's second floor concerning the history of naval war-gaming, part of a continuing exhibit on Naval War College history at the museum. Seen on the left is a blowup of the photograph of war-gaming at the college in 1914 (see p. 61). (Naval War College Museum.)

ENTRANCE TO THE MUSEUM. This 1988 photograph provides a close-up view of the sign at the entrance to the historic building. (Naval War College Museum.)

THE NAVAL WAR COLLEGE MUSEUM, C. 1983. Migrating Canada geese find friendly hospitality on the spacious lawn across from Founders Hall. (Naval War College Museum.)

THE *CONSTITUTION*. Named in honor of the Constitution of the United States in the naval war with France, the U.S. frigate *Constitution* served as Commodore Silas Talbot's flagship and as the flagship of Commodore Edward Preble in the war with Tripoli, participating in five engagements. The ship was nicknamed "Old Ironsides" for strength and good fighting in the War of 1812. Rebuilt in 1833, the ship served as a Naval Academy school ship from 1860 to 1865; was partially rebuilt in 1876; came to Newport in 1880 with other ships, when Capt. Stephen B. Luce commanded the Naval Apprentice System; and, except for one cruise, has been docked at Boston ever since. This model was donated to the Naval War College by retired Navy Lt. Cmdr. F.L. Higginson Jr. (Photograph by the author.)

PT Boats Exhibit. In 1986, the Naval War College Museum featured a display entitled "The Manufacture and Development of PT Boats." During World War II, PT boat training was conducted at nearby Melville, Rhode Island, seven miles north of Newport along Narragansett Bay. In the summer of 1943, at the height of operations, the Motor Torpedo Boat Squadrons Training Center, its official name, housed some 1,700 men. When the center closed in October 1945, it had graduated 2,017 officers and 12, 500 enlisted men. It was an elite, all-volunteer group who, unlike other military units at high risk, received no additional hazardous duty pay. John F. Kennedy was graduated from Melville in October 1942 and served in PT squadrons 2 and 5 in the Pacific theater. His wartime service was the subject of the film *PT 109*, with actor Cliff Robertson playing the young Navy lieutenant. (Naval War College Museum.)

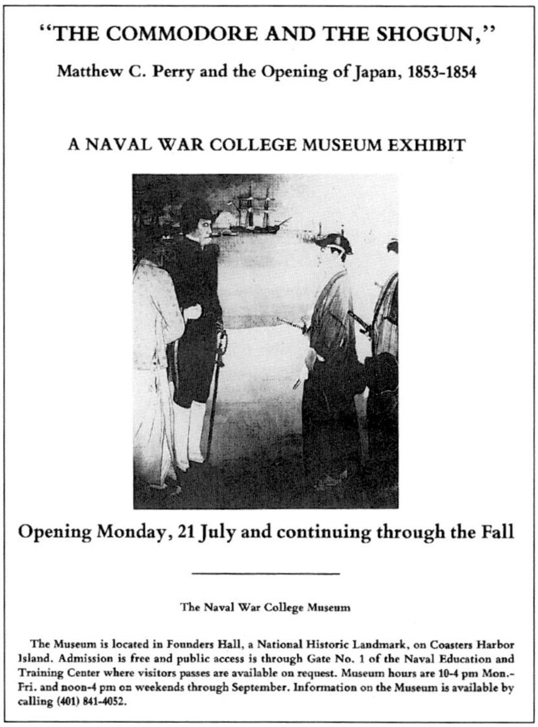

"The Commodore and the Shogun." This poster advertised a special exhibit on the historic opening of Japan by Commodore Oliver H. Perry. (Naval War College Museum.)

"THE SOVIET UNION. A PHOTOGRAPHIC ESSAY." The Naval War College Museum held a three-month exhibit of photographs of the Soviet Union by Rear Adm. Ronald J. Kurth, then college president. (Naval War College Museum.)

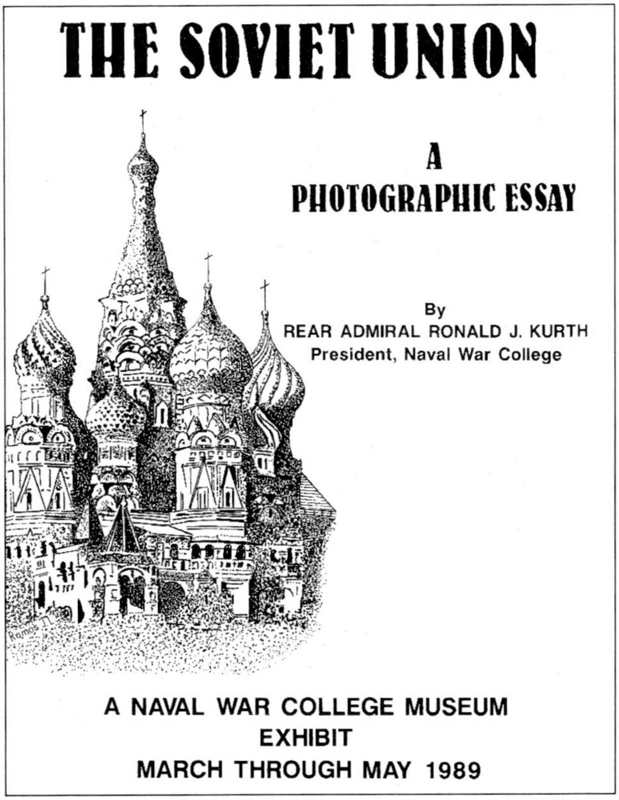

REAR ADM. RONALD J. KURTH. Born in Wisconsin, Ronald J. Kurth was in the Class of 1954 at the U.S. Naval Academy. Following a squadron tour and subsequent assignment as an instructor of Russian at the U.S. Naval Academy, Kurth entered Harvard University as a Navy-sponsored postgraduate student. In the meantime he also completed five years of aviation assignments with deployments to the Mediterranean and Vietnam. He first went to Moscow in 1971 to negotiate the Incidents at Sea Agreement. Thereafter, he served as the desk officer for the Soviet Union, East Europe, and Yugoslavia. In 1975, he went to Moscow as the naval attaché. Selected for rear admiral in 1981, he served in various capacities before returning to Moscow as the defense attaché. He assumed command of the Naval War College on August 11, 1987. (Naval War College Public Affairs Office.)

The Naval War College Museum announces a new exhibit:

THE EVOLUTION OF THE TORPEDO IN NARRAGANSETT BAY

Howell Torpedo ca. 1895, first propeller-driven torpedo used by the Fleet

The presentation is divided into two parts "The History of the Naval Torpedo Station, 1869-1951" and "Submarine Warfare in Transition," dealing in part with present day research and development at the Naval Underwater System Center.

NOVEMBER 1988 - APRIL 1989

The Naval War College Museum is located in Founders Hall, a National Historic Landmark, on Coasters Harbor Island, Newport, R.I. Admission is free and public access is through Gate No. 1 of the Naval Education and Training Center. Information is available by calling 841-4052.

TORPEDO DEVELOPMENT EXHIBIT. "The Evolution of the Torpedo in Narragansett Bay" was the theme of an exhibit that opened in November 1988. (Naval War College Museum.)

Announcing a new Naval War College Museum
Special Exhibit

NORMANDY

Paintings and Drawings of D-Day, 6 June 1944
from the Navy Art Collection, Washington, D.C.

COMMEMORATING

The commissioning of the USS *Normandy* (CG-60) at Newport, Rhode Island, 9 Dec 1989.

Opening Monday, 4 Dec 1989 and continuing through 16 Jan 1990.

The Naval War College Museum is located in Founders Hall, a National Historic Landmark, on Coasters Harbor Island, Newport, R.I. Admission is free and public access is through Gate No. 1 of the Naval Education and Training Center. Information is available by calling 841-4052.

"NORMANDY." Paintings and drawings of D-Day were displayed in a special Naval War College Museum exhibit in 1989. (Naval War College Museum.)

"**Kites in War and Peace.**" An exhibit featuring historical and contemporary kites opened on July 4, 1989. (Naval War College Museum.)

Signal Service Light, Naval War College. During the Spanish-American War in 1898, communities along the east coast feared enemy ships. To combat these fears, the government instituted a number of defensive measures, including the creation of the Coastal Signal Service. The service's mission was to warn the populace and the Navy of an impending attack. It maintained stations along the entire coast that were manned by state militia. This lighthouse lantern, on display at the Naval War College Museum, is believed to have been used by the Signal Service of Rhode Island. It was found c. 1900 in the cupola of the Naval War College's Luce Hall, shown in the picture hanging above it. The college played an important role in the establishment of the Coastal Signal Service, and members of the Naval War College staff occupied leadership positions in the state militia. (Photograph by the author.).

"TR's Navy" Exhibit. The establishment of permanent naval installations beyond the continental United States occurred during the administration of Pres. Theodore Roosevelt early in the 20th century. An exhibit called "TR's Navy" at the Naval War College Museum in 1997 focused, in part, on the creation of a naval base at Hawaii after the Spanish-American War. An addition to the exhibit was this 4-foot by 4-foot scale model of the Pearl Harbor Naval Base as it appeared just prior to the attack by Japanese aircraft on December 7, 1941, depicting the ultimate development of the advanced bases concept in the Pacific before World War II. The model is the work of Robert Brucci, second from right, who loaned it to the Naval War College for the exhibit. The model had previously been exhibited at the USS *Arizona* Memorial in Hawaii at the 50th anniversary of the Pearl Harbor attack. Shown with Brucci are, from left to right, retired Navy Cmdr. Alex Walsh, Mary Walsh, and retired Navy Capt. Herbert F. Rommel. Rommel was on the USS *Oklahoma*, one of the battleships sunk during the attack. Walsh was on the USS *Mahan*, DD 364, part of Adm. William Halsey's aircraft carrier task force that entered the harbor shortly after the attack and saw the carnage firsthand. Mrs. Walsh, at the time a young Navy wife living in the base area, also visited the scene in a successful search for her husband. (Courtesy Naval War College Foundation.)

THEODORE ROOSEVELT EXHIBIT. Capt. Mack Thomas, former deputy to the president of the Naval War College, and Tweed Roosevelt, representing the Theodore Roosevelt Association, unveil the bust of Pres. Theodore Roosevelt in the Naval War College Museum. The bust was presented to the museum by the association at the reception for the opening of "TR's Navy, Foundations of the Modern U.S. Fleet, 1883–1913." The presentation was made through the offices of the Naval War College Foundation. (Courtesy Naval War College Foundation.)

PANAMA CANAL. This scale model of the Panama Canal was part of the "TR's Navy" exhibit. (Naval War College Museum.)

Midshipman Luce. Stephen Bleecker Luce, the founder of the Naval War College, entered naval service at the age of 17 as a midshipman at the U.S. Naval Academy in Annapolis. He is shown here in a daguerreotype by Alexander James. The Naval War College Museum displays a copy on the third-floor stairwell. The original hangs in the Naval Academy commandant's house at Annapolis, Maryland. (U.S. Naval Academy Museum.)

WINTER SCENE. This winter scene of the Naval War College Museum was photographed in the 1980s. (Naval War College Museum.)

AN INVITATION TO THE
NAVAL WAR COLLEGE MUSEUM'S

Christmas Open House

Wednesday, 13 December
1 - 4 pm

Refreshments **Chamber music**

The Christmas Open House is a Naval War College Foundation supported event, and is held concurrently with the opening of the annual "Navy-Newport Artists and Art" exhibit.

The Naval War College Museum is located in Founders Hall (1820), a National Historic Landmark, on Coasters Harbor Island, Newport, R.I. Museum hours are 10–4 Monday-Friday, excluding holidays. Public access is through Gate No. 1 of the Naval Education and Training Center. Admission is free and information is available from 841-4052/1317.

CHRISTMAS OPEN HOUSE. This poster is typical of those advertising a Christmas open house, pretty much an annual tradition. (Naval War College Museum.)

Naval War College Museum, Luce Avenue, Front and East View. From the east side of the museum, Quarters A and AA, which serve as residences for the college provost and president, and other residences for college military staff in what is called "senior officer country" are a short walk up Bainbridge Road, on the right. (Naval War College Museum.)

View Across the Water. This contemporary view outside the front entrance of Founders Hall looks westward to the Newport Bridge over Narragansett Bay East Passage. (Photograph by the author.)

Seven

The College Presidents: A Reference List

Countless notable figures have served as president of the Naval War College, including the founder Cmdr. Stephen B. Luce; Alfred Thayer Mahan, the naval historian; Edward Clifford Kalbfus, who served three separate terms and for whom the street leading out of the Main Gate in Newport is named; James B. Stockdale, one of the longest internees as a POW of the Vietnam War; and Raymond A. Spruance, who was commander in chief in the Pacific in World War II. Some of the presidents have been singularly honored by having facilities named after them, reflected in such buildings as Luce, Mahan, Pringle, Spruance, and Conolly Halls.

A list is offered here as a reference for the reader on the various presidents of the college. The presidents are given in chronological order, with the president's name, rank while president, and dates of tenure at the Naval War College. The list includes acting (A) and interim (I) presidents—generally staff members who fulfilled the duties of the presidency temporarily and for short periods between detachments of a president and the arrival of his relief. Also included are several photographs of key Naval War College presidents, with brief descriptions of their backgrounds and aspects of their tenures in the position.

Stephen Bleecker Luce	Commodore	Oct. 6, 1884–June 22, 1886
Alfred Thayer Mahan	Captain	June 22, 1886–Jan. 12, 1889
Caspar Frederick Goodrich	Commander	Jan. 12, 1889–July 22, 1892
Alfred Thayer Mahan	Captain	July 22, 1892–May 10, 1893
Charles Herbert Stockton	Commander	May 10, 1893–Nov. 15, 1893
Henry Clay Taylor	Commander	Nov. 15, 1893–Dec. 31, 1896
Caspar Frederick Goodrich	Captain	Dec. 31, 1896–April 23, 1898

During the period from March 22, 1898, to November 2, 1898, the activities of the Naval War College were discontinued on account of the participation of the United States in the Spanish- American War.

Charles Herbert Stockton	Captain	Nov. 2, 1898–Oct. 25, 1900
French Ensor Chadwick	Rear Admiral	Oct. 25, 1900–Nov. 16, 1903
Charles Stillman Sperry	Captain	Nov. 16, 1903–May 24, 1906
John Porter Merrell	Rear Admiral	May 24, 1906– Oct. 6, 1909
Raymond Perry Rodgers	Rear Admiral	Oct. 6, 1909–Nov. 20, 1911
William Ledyard Rodgers	Captain	Nov. 20, 1911–Dec. 15, 1913
Austin Melvin Knight	Rear Admiral	Dec. 15, 1913–Feb. 16, 1917
William Sowden Sims	Captain	Feb. 16, 1917–April 28, 1917

During the period from 28 April 1917 to 11 April 1919 the activities of the Naval War College were discontinued on account of the participation of the United States in the World War.

William Sowden Sims	Rear Admiral	April 11, 1919–Oct. 15, 1922
Clarence Stewart Williams	Rear Admiral	Oct. 15, 1922–Sept. 5, 1925
William Veazie Pratt	Rear Admiral	Sept. 5, 1925–Sept. 17, 1927
Joel Robert Poinsett Pringle	Rear Admiral	Sept. 17, 1927–May 31, 1930
Harris Laning	Rear Admiral	June 16, 1930–May 14, 1933
Luke McNamee	Rear Admiral	June 3, 1933–June 15, 1934
Edward Clifford Kalbfus	Rear Admiral	June 15, 1934–June 15, 1936
Charles Philip Snyder	Rear Admiral	Jan. 2, 1937–May 27, 1939
Edward Clifford Kalbfus	Rear Admiral	Jun3 30, 1939–June 16, 1942
Edward Clifford Kalbfus	Rear Admiral	June 16, 1942–Nov. 2, 1942
William Satterlee Pye	Rear Admiral	Nov. 2, 1942–July 1, 1944
William Satterlee Pye	Rear Admiral	July 1, 1944–March 1, 1946
Raymond Ames Spruance	Admiral	March 1, 1946–July 1, 1948
Allen Edward Smith (A)	Rear Admiral	July 1, 1948–Nov. 1, 1948
Donald Bradford Beary	Vice Admiral	Nov. 1, 1948–May 28, 1950
Thomas Ross Cooley, (A)	Rear Admiral	May 28, 1950–Oct. 17, 1950
Harry D. Felt (A)	Captain	Oct. 17, 1950–Dec. 1, 1950
Richard L. Conolly	Vice Admiral	Dec. 1, 1950–Nov. 2, 1953
Thomas H. Robbins Jr. (A)	Rear Admiral	Nov. 2, 1953–May 3, 1954
Lynde D. McCormick	Rear Admiral	May 3, 1954–Aug. 16, 1956
Thomas H. Robbins Jr. (A)	Rear Admiral	Aug. 16, 1956–Sept. 4 , 1956

Thomas H. Robbins Jr.	Rear Admiral	Sept. 5, 1956–Aug. 1, 1957
Stuart H.Ingersoll	Vice Admiral	Aug.13 1957–June 30, 1960
Bernard L. Austin	Vice Admiral	June 30, 1960–July 31, 1964
Charles L. Melson	Vice Admiral	July 31, 1964–Jan.25, 1966
Francis E. Nuessle (A)	Rear Admiral	Jan. 25, 1966–Feb. 15, 1966
John Tucker Hayward	Vice Admiral	Feb. 15, 1966–Aug. 30, 1968
Richard G. Colbert	Vice Admiral	Aug. 30, 1968–Aug. 17, 1971
Benedict J. Semmes Jr.	Vice Admiral	Aug. 17, 1971–June 30, 1972
Stansfield Turner	Vice Admiral	June 30, 1972–Aug. 9, 1974
Julien J. LeBourgeois	Vice Admiral	Aug. 9, 1974–April 1, 1977
Huntington Hardisty	Rear Admiral	April 1, 1977–Oct. 13, 1977
James Bond Stockdale	Vice Admiral	Oct. 13, 1977–Aug. 22, 1979
Edward F. Welch Jr.	Rear Admiral	Aug. 22, 1979–Aug. 17, 1982
David L. Self (I)	Captain	Aug. 17, 1982–Oct. 14, 1982
James E. Service	Rear Admiral	Oct. 14, 1982–July 12, 1985
Robert B. Watts (I)	Captain	July 13, 1985–Aug. 13, 1985
Ronald F. Marryot	Rear Admiral	Aug. 13, 1985–Sept. 1, 1986
John A. Baldwin Jr.	Rear Admiral	Sept. 1, 1986–Aug. 11, 1987
Ronald J. Kurth	Rear Admiral	Aug. 11, 1987–July 17, 1990
Joseph C. Strasser	Rear Admiral	July 17, 1990–June 29, 1995
James R. Stark	Rear Admiral	June 29, 1995–July 24, 1998
Arthur K. Cebrowski	Vice Admiral	July 24, 1998–present

VICE ADM. WILLIAM S. PYE. Admiral Pye served as president of the Naval War College during the war years, as rear admiral from November 1942 to July 1944, then as vice admiral on the retired list from July 1, 1944, to March 1, 1946. He completed the four-year course at the Naval Academy in June 1901 and, after two years at sea—then required by law—he was commissioned ensign in the Navy on June 7, 1903. After various Fleet posts, he was ordered to the Naval War College and served on the staff from 1913 to 1915. He saw service in World War I and in later sea and shore posts, when, in July 1934, he was again ordered to the Naval War College as the senior member of the advanced class, inaugurated that year. As such, he served as assistant to the president in the establishment and conducting of the class. When Japan attacked Pearl Harbor, he was commander of Battleship Division Four and became acting commander in chief of the U.S. Pacific Fleet until the arrival of Admiral Nimitz. Pye commanded the Battle Force until appointment as president of the Naval War College. He was also named in charge of the Navy Operating Base. Pye designed and established the wartime command and preparatory staff courses at the college, and under his leadership over 600 Navy officers received advanced training. His success in improving the enlisted recruit and precommissioning training of the Naval Operating Base were also of major significance. His wife, Annie Etheldra Pye, was coauthor of the book *Navy Wife* (1942). (Naval War College Museum.)

VICE ADM. STUART H. INGERSOLL. A graduate of the U.S. Naval Academy, Ingersoll was said to have been both an old-time aviator and old-time destroyer man. For 15 years he served in carrier aviation. As a younger officer, he devoted time to the invention and development of the arresting gear that made aircraft carriers the great offensive weapon they were during World War II. In the latter part of the war, he commanded a fast carrier in Admiral Halsey's Fifth Fleet. He held a number of senior staff positions, including commandant of midshipmen at Annapolis. He served as president of the Naval War College from 1957 to 1960. (Naval War College Public Affairs Office.)

VICE ADM. CHARLES L. MELSON. In July 1964, Admiral Melson replaced Vice Adm. Bernard L. Austin as president of the Naval War College, serving until January 1966. Born in Richmond, Virginia, Melson attended the University of Richmond prior to appointment to the U.S. Naval Academy. He was commissioned ensign in June 1927. After the outbreak of war, he was assigned to headquarters of the commander in chief, U.S. Fleet, and in March 1942, he became assistant operations officer on the staff of commander in chief, U.S. Fleet. In September he assumed command of the USS *Champlin*, winning Legion of Merit, Commendation Ribbon, and Bronze Star awards. He won further commendations and the Bronze Star medal as operations officer and assistant chief of staff to commander destroyers, U.S. Atlantic Fleet. From July 1947 to May 1948, he attended the senior course at the Naval War College, where he remained on duty as staff until July 1949. He then took command of Destroyers Squadron Twenty, USS *Barton*, flagship, and a year later became administrative aide to the superintendent of the U.S. Naval Academy. Following commendatory service in Korea, Melson served in such leadership positions as command of Cruiser Division Four and as superintendent of the U.S. Naval Academy with additional duty as commandant Severn River Naval Command. He assumed command of the First Fleet with rank of vice admiral in July 1960 and commanded the U.S. Taiwan Defense Command from 1962 to 1964, when he became president of the Naval War College (see pp. 71-72). (Naval War College Public Affairs Office.)

VICE ADM. JOHN TUCKER HAYWARD. A native of New York City, Admiral Hayward was in the enlisted service until he received appointment to the U.S. Naval Academy, from which he graduated with a degree in electrical engineering. As a naval aviator, he amassed over 14,000 hours of flying time and 310 carrier landings. Heavily involved in research, development, and testing of aeronautical equipment, he organized, trained, and commanded the Navy's first heavy attack squadron and was the first naval aviator to land heavy attack aircraft onboard a carrier. A member of the Manhattan Project, he also had extensive command experience including commander Antisubmarine Warfare Force in the Pacific. In February 1966, he became the 32nd president of the Naval War College. He has been honored by a D.Sc. degree from the University of Portland and a D.LL.degree from Providence College. He was awarded the Distinguished Flying Cross four times including once by the army, five Air Medals, the Legion of Honor from France, the Order of the British Empire, the Royal Order of the Brazilian Southern Cross, and the Knight Commander of the Order of Merit of the Republic of Italy. Hayward was awarded the Robert Dexter Conrad Scientific Award for outstanding physicists, the only military recipient of this honor. He retired with his wife, Lili Hayward, to Newport, Rhode Island. (Public Affairs Office, Naval War College.)

VICE ADM. RICHARD G. COLBERT. A native of Brownsville, Pennsylvania, and a 1937 graduate of the U.S. Naval Academy, Admiral Colbert served sea duty on the USS *Yorktown*, CV-13, and the USS *Barker*, DD-213. When the latter moved from the Asiatic Fleet in 1942 to the Atlantic Fleet, Colbert became the ship's commanding officer. In 1944, he reported as commanding officer of the USS *Meade*, DD-602, and in June 1948, he was ordered to England as aide and flag secretary to Adm. R. L. Connolly. Following other major assignments, including two years aboard the USS *Albany*, CA-123, as executive officer, he was ordered to Newport as a student in the Naval War College. Just prior to completion of the course in the spring of 1956, then Captain Colbert was assigned to organize and act as director of a new course for senior free world naval officers. This course was established by Adm. Arleigh Burke, chief of naval operations (see p. 80) in August 1956 and included students from up to 30 allied and friendly countries. In 1968, following other service posts in Washington, D.C., and at sea and with the rank of vice admiral, Colbert became president of the Naval War College. He served also as the first director of the Naval Command College for international officers and based on his ideas, a second international program, for middle-grade officers, was inaugurated after his presidency. In 1971, he was named chief of staff to the supreme allied commander in the Atlantic, and in June 1972, in the rank of admiral, became commander in chief of Allied Forces in Southern Europe. (Public Affairs Office, Naval War College and Navy Office of Information.)

Vice Adm. Stansfield Turner. A native of Highland Park, Illinois, Admiral Turner entered Amherst College in 1941 and transferred to the U.S. Naval Academy in 1943. At graduation he was the commander of the brigade of midshipmen. Following a year of sea duty, he was appointed a Rhodes Scholar and entered Oxford University in 1947, where he studied philosophy, political science, and economics. In the 1950s and 1960s, he served in various sea and shore commands, was selected for rear admiral in May 1970, assumed command of Cruiser-Destroyer Flotilla Eight and of a carrier task force of the Sixth Fleet in September 1970 aboard the USS *Independence* in the Mediterranean. In 1972, the Senate confirmed his nomination to vice admiral and assignment as president of the Naval War College. He became the college's 36th President on June 30, 1972, the youngest flag officer and only Rhodes Scholar ever to assume the presidency of the college. Turner expanded the college faculty and revamped the academic program around faculty-led seminars in three courses which still form the basis of the college's curriculum: strategy and policy, defense economics and decision making, and naval operations. Also he inaugurated a second international program, the Naval Staff College, for middle-grade international officers. (Public Affairs Office, Naval War College.)

Rear Adm. James R. Stark. During his final year at the U.S. Naval Academy, Admiral Stark earned a Fulbright Scholarship and spent most of his first year in the Navy as a student at the University of Vienna, doing postgraduate study in history. He served staff posts on several destroyers and in 1981 took command of the guided missile frigate *Julius A. Furer*, FFG 6, then command of the cruiser *Leahy*, CG 6, and later served as commander of NATO's standing naval forces in the Atlantic. Ashore, he was an advisor to senior decision makers, including the President of the United States. The Navy assigned him to Medford, Massachusetts, to earn a Ph.D. in international law and diplomacy from the Fletcher School at Tufts University. Stark served as president of the Naval War College for three years, from June 1995 to July 1998, during a period of intense change and growth for the college. He aggressively reached out to the Fleet through the college's nonresident programs by making seminar courses more widely available and revising the correspondence program to better fit busy career paths. At Newport he was one of the principal architects of the reorganization and growth of the college, including the start of construction for a Strategic Maritime Research Center in October 1997. The $16 million project features a television studio, administrative offices, and a state-of-the-art electronic naval war-gaming simulation facility. (Courtesy Naval War College Foundation.)

Vice Adm. Arthur K. Cebrowski. The Navy's expert on "network-centric" warfare, Admiral Cebrowski became the 47th president of the Naval War College during a change of command ceremony at Colbert Plaza on July 24, 1998. In his career he commanded a fighter squadron, an air wing, an amphibious helicopter carrier, and the aircraft carrier *Midway*. He has also taken leadership roles ashore, in examining the concepts and developing tools of the high speed, networked information age. When he became president, he was the first three-star admiral to lead the school since Vice Adm. James B. Stockdale stepped down from the post in 1979. The role of the college was changing dramatically, in facilities, courses, and administration. In August 1998, a flag-rank position was created, and Rear Adm. Peter A.C. Long took over as the first provost. In an address to an incoming class, Admiral Cebrowski called the War College the Navy's "intellectual center of gravity." He promised to reshape the school for the information age, accepting its proud tradition but facing the current era of continuing change and directing its attention toward the future. Adding to the new role and mission of the Naval War College was a new command—the Navy warfare development command—headed by Rear Adm. Bernard J. Smith. The new command was established to partner with the fleet to act as a catalyst for innovation within naval doctrine for effectively shaping the future capabilities of the Navy. (Public Affairs Office, Naval War College.)

United States Naval War College Coat of Arms

The wavy white and blue bars at the bottom of the shield represent water. The trident rising from it symbolizes mastery of naval activities. The three tines of the trident allude to an understanding of naval warfare at sea, in the air, and on land. The pilot wheel alludes to the mission of the Naval War College, education in naval warfare. The eight spokes refer to honor, duty, leadership, command, strategy, tactics, logistics, and weapons. The laurel wreath is for achievement of the mission. The motto is "Victory Through Sea Power."

ACKNOWLEDGMENTS

A considerable part of this book is derived from photographs in the collection of the Naval War College Museum, and the work overall owes much to the help and courtesy of the museum staff. Director Anthony S. Nicolosi gave unstinting support and arranged for a number of prints, including several from Naval Education and Training Center headquarters displays, and helped in resolving questions of dates and personnel. To museum curator Robert M. Cembrola, this book owes much. Not only did he allow the use of his office for compiling notes and working the photograph files, he was always ready to answer questions and provide helpful information on Naval War College history, events, and buildings, including the museum and its exhibits. Dr. Evelyn Cherpak, Naval War College archivist, arranged for the viewing of numerous documents and other holdings.

Retired Navy Capt. Elizabeth Wylie, executive director of the Naval War College Foundation, and her staff gave assistance in locating photographs and news stories that appeared in *Foundation Notes*, *Naval War College Review*, and other foundation releases. The Naval War College Public Affairs Office provided pictures of the presidents, as well as related news releases and other information. For help with questions on photographs and related graphics, thanks goes to Rita M. Sullivan, Todd Rushton, and Jeffrey Owens. Personnel at Arcadia were most helpful, especially Amy Sutton, senior editor in Dover, New Hampshire, who conscientiously watched over the manuscript and offered suggestions for improving text and layout along the way. For assistance and advice with computer matters, appreciation is due to grandson J. Michael Wyld-Chirico of Attleboro, Massachusetts.

To my wife, Norma, go more than the usual thanks for her thoughtful comments on pictures and captions and especially for her patience as the length of time for gathering and preparing material extended into vacation travel and other planning.

The book has been reviewed in prepublication layout by the Naval War College Public Affairs Office and Naval War College Foundation. All material from Navy sources is cleared for release, and credits for the source of photographs are given in the captions.